Contents

For the rescued and the rescuers,
who in their various ways have
kept going back in.

Paul Brown trained as a geologist in Sydney, and is an expert on ocean floor rocks at Gundagai. In 1981, after five years in student theatre, he founded one of Australia's foremost community theatre companies, Death Defying Theatre, now Urban Theatre Projects. In 1985 he turned to writing, and wrote *Coal Town*, a play about social and political struggle in mining towns for performance on Queensland football fields. He has since worked as a freelance playwright, often in community contexts, and on drama and documentary films as writer, producer and songwriter. His community plays include *Kahkwa Hakawati*, made with Sydney's Arab Australian community about the Gulf War, and the riverbank extravaganza *Murray River Story*, which dealt with environmental problems of the Murray River. His films include the screen version of *Aftershocks* and an episode for the ABC series *Naked: Stories of Men*. For two years, Paul was Campaign Manager for Greenpeace Australia, and he is currently a lecturer in the School of Science and Technology Studies at the University of New South Wales, where he teaches and researches Environmental Studies while continuing to write plays and films.

Since 1974 the workers cultural action committee has produced collaborative arts projects of the highest standard. What began as a voluntary sub-committee of Newcastle Trades Hall Council is now a separate arts and cultural broker with its feet firmly grounded in the values and principles of the union movement. The committee has managed many different projects on a variety of themes: youth employment, people with disabilities and traditional workers' celebrations like May Day. From 1997 to 1999 the committee initiated the Molten Arts Project involving over 200 employees in a range of artworks about the closure of the Newcastle Steelworks. They have presented other performances and publications, designed posters and organised cultural actions. Their work is accessible, innovative, challenging and community-based. It involves different ways of artist and community working together to form an art product indicative of the community and its culture. They believe in a fair and just society where everyone has the right to express themselves in a cultural form appropriate to them.

The workers cultural action committee is funded by the Community Cultural Development Fund of the Australia Council, the federal government's arts funding and advisory body, the NSW Government through the Ministry for the Arts and assisted through in-kind support from Newcastle Trades Hall Council.

Australia Council for the Arts

nsw arts MINISTRY FOR THE

NTHC NEWCASTLE TRADES HALL COUNCIL

Aftershocks

Paul Brown and the Workers Cultural Action Committee

CURRENCY PRESS
SYDNEY

CURRENCY PLAYS

First published in 1993
by Currency Press Pty Ltd,
PO Box 2287, Strawberry Hills, NSW, 2012, Australia
enquiries@currency.com.au
www.currency.com.au

Revised edition published 2001

Reprinted 2009, 2011, 2013, 2014, 2015, 2017, 2018, 2020, 2022, 2023

Cataloguing-in-publication data for this title is available from the National Library of Australia website: www.nla.gov.au

Typeset by Dean Nottle for Currency Press.
Printed by Fineline Print + Copy Services, Revesby, NSW.
Cover design by Katy Wall for Currency Press.
Cover photograph by Steve Tickner.

Aftershocks—Ten Years In The Making

Paul Brown

Conceived by the Workers Cultural Action Committee as a community arts project in response to the 1989 Newcastle earthquake, Aftershocks *has been a set of taped interviews, a stage play, a touring production, fragments of radio, the subject of popular and academic writing, and a feature film.*

This second edition of the play script is being published almost exactly ten years after the first production of the play by the Workers Cultural Action Committee and Hunter Valley Theatre Company. Writer Paul Brown describes the various stages of the project.[1]

LOCAL STORIES, NATIONAL CULTURE

Aftershocks began life as conversations between staff, members and friends of the Newcastle Workers Club. It is gutsy, bloody and humorous, and it tells what these people did on the day of the Newcastle earthquake when their club was reduced to a pile of twisted rubble, and several of their friends died. It is a local story.

In forging national culture, the best and most important stories *are* local. They rise like rebellions from real events in neighbourhoods and in workplaces. They are told, then shaped by retellings until they are lore. They can colonise a nation's cultural traditions from within.

Aftershocks has been claimed as a valued Australian literary and dramatic work of some national significance,[2] and in a way this reinforces national 'ownership' of the real event—the Newcastle earthquake. This could just be because it was the only Australian earthquake to have taken human life (there were twelve deaths). But the play, and the film, also speak of some universal themes: in disaster, how do people react and assume leadership? How does healing occur after loss of life? How do we express our experience of crisis through language? And arguably this *is* an event that we should all 'own', for the answers it gives to these questions and for what it therefore tells us about ourselves.

SBS Television, which funded the film version, first screened *Aftershocks* on 31 December 1998, a few days after the ninth anniversary of the Newcastle earthquake. For the next two years they screened the film on or close to the anniversary date, and in this way it played across Australia simultaneously as an entertainment and a memorial.

ORIGINS

The days of immediate crisis following the earthquake on 28 December 1989 had been documented in many ways by the time of the official Inquiry halfway through 1990. What was poorly understood at the time was the extent to which the aftermath would be painful for many, perhaps more full of crisis than the day the earthquake struck. Sluggishness by governments and insurance companies, insurance rorts, lack of funding for emergency reconstruction, dislocation from homes or workplaces and grief all hit home. There was a desire for closure in Newcastle—for the story of the earthquake to end, for it to be filed away and forgotten, for rebuilding to proceed quickly. But for many reasons this could not happen, and for some people, a 'normal life' would not be achieved for ten years.

In mid 1990 in response to this situation, Newcastle's Workers Cultural Action Committee (WCAC) proposed a play about the earthquake, to put on stage the perspective of people involved with the collapse of the Newcastle Workers Club.

In Newcastle, there have long been intimate connections and overlap of personnel and interests between the Trades Hall, the Workers Club and the WCAC (itself a Trades Hall sub-committee). A number of staff and students of Newcastle University and many individual artists also have affiliations with the WCAC, and together these organisations and individuals make up a network concerned with cultural development among Newcastle workers and their families. This follows a long tradition. For example, the club's Entertainment Unit provided vaudeville performances for and by club members in the 1950s; and in the twenty-seven years of work by the WCAC a wide range of arts activities has been under the auspices of the trade union movement—murals, banners, choirs, videos, plays, processions, film screenings and more. Recent work has included cultural activities associated with the closure of BHP in Newcastle.

Aftershocks was conceived as part of this continuum, with the premise that it should be a community arts project arising from and owned by the Workers Club and its people. A common challenge for such work is maintaining community control, in particular the rights an individual has over her or his own story. In community theatre the licensing of stories for use by a company of actors had been a haphazard affair before about 1990. Typically there was an unwritten assumption that material developed in a drama workshop could go forward into performance, or that a writer could collect stories and weave them into a text he or she then owned. Reformists were calling for much greater community control and protection of copyright and moral rights. They proposed using steering committees to guide the work at several stages, release forms to preserve the storyteller's control, and feedback and checking processes to demonstrate what was being done with the material and to allow power of veto to the storyteller. For *Aftershocks* we set out to use all of these mechanisms.[3]

The WCAC had employed me as Community Writer in Residence in late November 1990 with funding from the Literature Board of the Australia Council. WCAC also put together a team of eight researchers. These included David Watt (who also undertook a dramaturgical role in the project and went on to co-direct the first production of the play), Carole Collet, Carol Myers and Vanessa Hutchins, who had all been involved with previous WCAC projects; also David Owens from the committee itself, Julie Pavlou Kirri who was at the time WCAC organiser, and Newcastle actor Paul Makeham who subsequently appeared in the original production. A key member of the team was club board member Bob Phillips, who wrote a history of the Workers Club.[4]

A steering group of ten trade unionists and club personnel met to provide essential information to the research team and to suggest directions for the play. This group included Trades Hall Secretary Peter Barrack, club Secretary / Manager Wayne Dean, Liquor Trades unionist Howard Gibson, and Waterside Workers leader Eddie Seymour, also a member of the Workers Club board. Members of this group made themselves available for ongoing consultation about the project, and most also became interviewees. More informal steerage for the project came in the form of daily feedback from both storytellers and interviewers.

SETTING A PATH

The first meetings of the steering group and research team agreed that some constraints were needed since almost every Newcastle resident has a story to tell about the earthquake. By the time the project began in earnest, in mid December 1990, the following subject areas and themes had been defined:

1. The day of the quake, 28 December 1989, and the collapse of the club. The perspective of the workers in the club, of the patrons, the rescuers, the unionists involved. Feats of bravery, danger, loss of life, fear, anger, surprise, humour. And several other angles: people not in Newcastle desperate to get home (the sense of being blocked out, imagining the worst), the emergency services, the use of radio as communication.
2. The aftermath, from several perspectives. The club staff who lost friends, whose union boss deserted them, who lost their jobs. The insurance of pay packets. The dispute over the demolition firms, the club demolished, people with housing problems.
3. 'Ownership' of the earthquake. Authority on the day of the quake—by virtue of expertise, by virtue of established hierarchy. Barricades in the city. Ownership of the story of the quake—by the press, by the politicians, by the people of Newcastle.
4. The idea of 'club' (and this to be the heart of the piece). Dislocation for the trade union movement and the undermining of the long-standing traditions of the club. What has been the importance of the club for the community of Newcastle? Has the postwar idea of a working-people's club run its course? What will be the new relationship between the club and the community? The rise of the new club.

5. A struggle not yet won. No romantic conclusion about community spirit conquering all. Our characters should come out of all this with great dignity, some of them as heroes or heroines, but there should be no pretence that this means the earthquake is over. The aftermath contains many lessons about the horror of human behaviour as well, and the play should take account of structural factors that continue to divide the community. The play's ending is probably about coping with ongoing chaos rather than defeating it all together.[5]

VERBATIM THEATRE

Derek Paget defines the British tradition of 'Verbatim Theatre' as 'that form of documentary drama which employs (largely or exclusively) tape recorded material from the "real life" originals of the characters and events to which it gives dramatic shape'. He has further characterised verbatim as a theatre in which 'the firmest of commitments is made by the company to the use of vernacular speech', and as work based on 'painstaking, protracted and scrupulous use of historical evidence'.[6]

Most British verbatim theatre has been minimalist in terms of sets, props and costumes, and has relied on simple storytelling for its power. Shows have been used as celebration (of a locality, of past events) or to deal with current controversy (for example a show about the 1984-5 British Miners' Strike). As Paget points out, much documentary theatre has been oppositional to mainstream views, aiming to give voice to people who have been otherwise disenfranchised, and to dramatise events which are invisible to, or misinterpreted by, mainstream media. Such intentions are certainly behind the *Laramie Project*, which Belvoir Street Theatre produced in 2001 and which has been widely compared with *Aftershocks*. It uses verbatim techniques to unravel why a young homosexual man was murdered in a small US town.[7]

In Australia by 1990, much use had been made of oral-history principles in community theatre projects. Often the cornerstone of these projects was the active participation by all those in a particular community with stories to tell. This participation has occurred in many ways: through the research efforts of a company of actors, by script writing workshops open to all comers, by theatre workshops designed to explore local stories as drama, and not least by having enormous casts perform the material.

The *Murray River Story*, *Promised Land* and *Two Cities*, all projects of the Murray River Performing Group, are examples of community theatre work in which local stories were the fundamental building blocks of the drama, and they formed reference points for *Aftershocks*.[8] However, *Aftershocks* is one of the few Australian plays, and we think the first, to be entirely based on taped interviews, and, with very rare exceptions, to use only words spoken by the original storytellers. In *Two Cities* a small number of speeches are taken verbatim from taped interviews, but the vast majority of stories were adapted in workshop. This process of adaptation can be, of course, the best way to dramatise a story. The question of whether to use material verbatim will have a different answer in every project.

In *Aftershocks*, various options for dramatising the stories from the club were kept open until quite late in the drafting process. But the power of the original stories, told simply, convinced us to pursue a 'pure verbatim' approach. There was considerable confidence in 'verbatim' from the two people who went on to direct the original production: David Watt, who knew of verbatim plays in Canada and Britain, and Brent McGregor who was then Chair of WCAC.

INTERVIEWS: COMMITMENT TO THE VERNACULAR

Bob Phillips had recorded interviews about the quake with club workers in January 1990, some three weeks after the quake. The power of these first-hand stories from club staff involved in the collapse of their workplace acted as a spur to those working on the project and their testimony remains one of the strongest influences on the play.[9]

The research team recorded twenty-three new interviews. Some followed up, one year later, Bob Phillips' initial interviews.[10] Other taped interviews were available from various sources, including; for example, the Sociology Department of Newcastle University.[11] The interviewers sought opinions and anecdotes from each participant, relating to the previously agreed subject areas.

Interviews were recorded at broadcast quality; the duration is typically about 45 minutes, although some last more than two hours. The licensing of stories was negotiated using a release form which guaranteed the interviewees certain rights and allowed them to decide how their stories might be used not only within the project, but under future circumstances. (The release form is included as an Appendix.) Importantly, the steering group had already anticipated the possibility that the project might become a film, and it was agreed that this would require further negotiation.

The choice of interviewees was helped by the steering group, but it also reflected the intuition of the researchers. It is important to note that club staff had by this stage told and re-told their stories many times—to each other, to the press, to counsellors, and to an Inquiry. Their stories had been re-shaped by the perspectives of their workmates, since to some extent each person relied on details they learnt from someone else to help unravel what had clearly been a chaotic and incomprehensible experience. A commonsense view prevailed about who had important stories to tell, and about how those stories should be represented. Certain staff members were known to be reluctant to speak about their experiences and the research team did not attempt to persuade them to participate.

The key to the success of each interview was the one-to-one relationship established between interviewer and interviewee. The researchers knew well the people they were interviewing. Almost a year after the quake, David Owens interviewed John Constable at Newcastle Trades Hall, where they locked themselves away in the kitchen with the tape recorder for three hours. David and John were both cleaners at the club, and they sat there poring over the club plans, going through details of the collapse as two workmates might over morning tea. Julie Pavlou Kirri interviewed Eddie Seymour, whom she knew from Trades Hall committees, and the text bears all the hallmarks of this established relationship. When Carol Myers made the remarkable interview with Jenny Mathews (who was trapped by the leg after the collapse), the pair knew each other as neighbours from Stockton. All the interviews in some way depended on the dynamic produced by such intimate relationships.

It was certainly a significant time to be conducting interviews. The Governor General laid the foundation stone for the new club on 19 December, and ceremonies marking the anniversary of the earthquake took place on 28 December. These events were uppermost in the minds of club workers involved in the *Aftershocks* project and arguably gave the interviews a particular intensity. The resulting tapes range widely across events before, during and after the earthquake.[12]

MAKING THE PLAY

The research team completed transcriptions of the interviews in January 1991, and the development of a 'rough draft' for the play began. The writer's job in this phase was to structure extracts from the transcripts into dramatic form. This began with a 'first cull' of material, reducing some 250 pages of transcript by about half. The consultation with the research team, the steering group and the interviewees continued throughout this process. Not only were form and content under constant review, but also production logistics. So for example, the decision to create a play which could 'travel' meant crafting a reasonably tight piece for no more than six performers that could be performed in almost any space.

Once transcribed, the interviews were broken down into grabs, each grab constituting a discreet story fragment. These were trimmed if necessary to enhance the dramatic effect, without changing the intent or mood of the story, and certainly without altering the unique grammatical constructions that belonged to each speaker. The one exception were words that reflected hesitation due entirely to the interview process, for example some, though not all, of the 'ums' and 'ahs'. We added to the transcripts many of the sighs, laughs and other non-word sounds that accompanied the storytelling on tape. It is indeed the repetitions, convolutions, pauses, malapropisms, idiom, vocabulary and non-word sounds that make each character's voice as distinctive as a fingerprint, and we were determined to retain all these characteristics.

Grabs were then juxtaposed to make up scenes. For example the words of club workers Margaret Turnbull and Kerry Ingram were combined to build a picture of events on the footpath outside the club:

MARG: (MT4) We're just trying to stop bleeding with our bare hands, type of thing... which is, you know, friggin' difficult.

KERRY: (MT10) One lady that has a cut, I'm not exactly sure where it is, somewhere down between her fingers, and it's cut an artery or a vein or something, and every time her heart pumps, it's just pumping out. And we're actually holding her hand, squeezing it with our fingers, trying to stop her bleeding to death in front of us.

MARG: (MT10) And all she's worried about is her husband. She keeps saying that her husband was sitting in the car in the carpark. We've got no way of knowing whether he is or not. But we're holding her hand so tightly to try and stop this bleeding, the ring on her finger is cutting into her finger where we're squeezing it.

KERRY: (MT11) She just keeps saying, 'Let it go, let it go'. But we can't. If we let it go she'll bleed to death in front of us.

MARG: (MT10) My uniform is all covered in blood.[13]

The rough draft was assembled around two main thematic strands: one about how people cope with disaster, the other about the importance of the club to the Newcastle community. Tentative through-lines were developed around concerns that participants had in common—for example, each person's reflection on the fate of workmates who were trapped and killed, or the details of life-saving actions by a comrade. The sense of 'the club' was conveyed in scenes of recollection about club history as well as through people's attitude to their jobs or their relationships with club patrons.

FIRST PUBLIC READING

We presented a reading of the rough draft, as a work in progress, early in February 1991: the first test of the material in front of an audience and a means for the community to maintain control over the work. The performance took place in the Playhouse Theatre in Newcastle before an audience that included club workers who had given their stories, members of the Workers Cultural Action Committee, the project steering committee, theatre workers, staff from Newcastle University Drama and Sociology departments, and others.

There was half a play. The performance by the eight researchers, who read from loose-leaf folders, took 50 minutes. Staging was extremely simple, with basic blocking, no costumes or props. Each reader/actor played two or three different real-life characters—the people they themselves had interviewed—with no attempt to mimic the real person's physical or linguistic mannerisms, other that what the words on the page dictated. As far as 'acting' goes, the readers simply attempted to tell stories to the audience.

This reading confirmed that the use of verbatim speech was extremely potent. The comments of those present reveal how oral history material works as theatre and the power of language to convey image. As one put it 'The strength of this is clearly in the language. And you've gotta keep that ... people are projecting these very strong images of dance floors in the middle of the air, and slabs, and poker machines, and buildings wrapped in things. All those are very powerful dramatic images'.[14]

Another common response was to approve the simplicity of the work. One interviewer said 'I just like people on stage telling stories. No books, no nothing. Just them, telling the story'. For interviewees, their own stories fed back seemed moving and entertaining. Howard Gibson said, 'It came across to me, being a participant in the Workers Club at the time, absolutely spot on. I could pick the characters straight away. Course I've got a bit of an edge as far as it goes'.

Most people recognised a unique personal experience that had universal relevance: 'The things about each of those real people that come out is I think what makes it universal. And that's what a lot of people outside Newcastle can most relate to. They probably know someone like that. Especially in Australia perhaps', and 'It could be about the earthquake in Scorpie in '61, it could be about in San Francisco in '89. But it was in Australia. You've documented it word by word, and there's no way you're gonna get around the Australiana of it'.

The integrity of the process had been important for many in the audience: 'Tonight's illusion, for us, was that you were honest people giving honest accounts from people who were just doing that: telling us a story … There is that sense that you're privileged to be given these stories, and the people handling them, even the way they handle the scripts, is a reflection that they're aware that they're in privileged positions'. Some also reacted to the material as 'alternative': 'This to me read of true stories ... To me it has a non-media perspective … exploring the way the media presents stories like this, and the way real people see them. If you put it on television with the CNN presentation, it becomes incredibly trivial, and just doesn't have the emotional power that this has'.

Above all, perhaps, it did seem to address the principle objective of the project, to make a play relevant to contemporary Newcastle: 'If there was an audience of Newcastle people watching I'm sure you'll have most of them in tears by halfway through. I definitely felt very teary. For me, not having been into [the centre of] Newcastle on the day, I relate very strongly to the passage about wanting to go in there and see what had happened. And I think it painted a picture beautifully for people who weren't able to go there'. The material seemed to spark a re-working of events for the audience, and even to provide a necessary ritual for some: 'I felt very solemn after that reading, actually, and just the very simplicity of things is something that is really important. I didn't go to any of the [official] ceremonies or anything, and the solemnity of tonight's reading was a really nice bit of therapy, and I'm sure that would be the way it would work for a Newcastle audience in particular'.

A BLUEPRINT FOR PRODUCTION

A full version of the *Aftershocks* script was completed in February 1991, shortly after the reading of the work in progress. Further script development took place during the original Newcastle season. In reflecting the preferences of the first-reading audience, the new draft advanced the rough draft in two important ways. First, it pursued further than we originally intended the notion of a very simple staging, and with a cast that functions primarily as a group of storytellers rather than as characters. Second, it gave a greater sense of the politics and history of the Newcastle Workers Club by using more stories about what the club meant to its workers and to the community. Characters such as Melba Middleby and Stefo Natsou were brought into sharper focus.

The selection and placement of speeches conformed to a structure largely invented by the writer, but at the same time the selection reflected the central concerns and the mood of individual interviews. A small number of intersecting stories functioned as through-lines, thereby establishing a number of 'through characters'. The work relationship of John Constable and his supervisor Lyn Brown, for example, takes on a mother-son quality. In the script this is brought out in the story of Lyn's dramatic rescue by John:

LYN: (LB6) They virtually just held it in mid-air, and John climbed the ladder, with the guys holding it, and he jumped over into my office, and just grabbed hold of me. Don't ask me how I got over to the ladder, but I had to get over to the ladder…

(LB26) And he just kept on talking, going from one thing to another. He was still very hyped up, but when he reached me he seemed to settle a little bit more. He probably felt that the shoe was on the other foot… at the moment he was probably able to do something for me for a change.

JOHN: (JC57) I said, 'I'll go first and you can come down sort of in front of me'. Anyway, she's… I've gone down, and she couldn't get down fast enough. [*Laughing*] I thought I was gonna go right up her skirt.

LYN: (LB7) And John manoeuvred me down this ladder, and they said, 'Step out onto this ledge'. I put one foot out, and then the ledge went, so I had to get back on the ladder, and we went down a bit further… that's where they jammed the door in, between the carpet and some rubble. And a workman was standing behind that, and I had to jump over to the… to the door, and so he had his arms out, you know, and it was only a little space that I had to jump over to.

(LB9) And all of a sudden I saw these stairways sticking out from nowhere. I had to jump around onto that, then. And then John followed me down the ladder. He followed me down the ladder, and he just… when we got halfway down the stairs, you know, he just sorta grabbed hold of me, and sort of, you know, went to pieces.

JOHN: (JC11) She give me a big cuddle, and I give her a cuddle, a pretty tight one.

He laughs, and enacts breathing heavily in the cuddle.

Important through-lines were also constructed around the most deeply felt concerns the storytellers shared—for example, each person's reflection on the fate of their workmates who were trapped or killed. Other stories are short-lived within individual scenes, and/or 'nested' one within another. Wherever multiple perspectives on the same incident are available, such an incident becomes a 'node' within the play, a point in time to which the narrative may return before branching along a new path. The exit of club worker Howard Gibson from the building is one example.

SEASONS OF THE PLAY

The play was ultimately devised for six actors who in the mode of storytellers use the verbatim dialogue to construct the stories of the staff and friends of the Workers Club. It was first performed in a three-week season beginning 12 November 1991 at the Newcastle Playhouse, presented by the WCAC with the assistance of the Hunter Valley Theatre Company.[15]

The preparations for this season were a critical time for finalising the structure of the play and bringing it 'to length'. (*Aftershocks* is constructed as two fifty minute halves.) We also experimented with the text in some places. In one or two scenes we brought the stories into the 'present' by changing the tense of verbs—we felt that the sacrifice of verbatim was worth it for the heightened drama. We also created tiny 'signposts' at the start and close of scenes—mostly captions such as 'Howard and Elaine's Story'. (See the head of Scene 3.)

The Playhouse staging was extremely simple. The list of scenes was painted on the back wall and, although each played two or three characters, the cast told the stories without a costume change. For props they relied on six chairs that served primarily as 'home bases' for storytellers, and were occasionally used to create a sense of the wreckage.[16] Photographs of the club, historical ones, and others showing the earthquake devastation, were displayed in the foyer.

There will never be another season quite like the first one. The performers, all of them Newcastle actors, had an intimate knowledge of the people whose stories they were telling and of the impact of the earthquake on their own community. Many though not all of the interviewees attended the play. The actors encountered them face to face during the performance and afterwards in the foyer. These experiences were very emotional.

By the mid 1990s, the play had been taken up by a number of theatre companies across the country. The steering group for

Aftershocks always wanted it to travel. After its initial Newcastle season, the play toured within the Hunter Valley. It played at Belvoir Street Theatre in Sydney in 1993, and was included in the Melbourne Theatre Company's 1995 season. Numerous schools, university theatre companies and other groups also took it up. Brent McGregor staged a reading of *Aftershock* in Brisbane in 1993 while he was Director of Street Arts.

The Belvoir Street production directed by Neil Armfield was the springboard for taking the play beyond Newcastle. It featured Jeremy Sims as John Constable, a role he later played in the film. John and most of the other interviewees have closely followed the play's fortunes, becoming involved as advisors in the rehearsal process and in promoting the major seasons.

The verbatim approach has prompted audiences, actors, directors and writers alike to grapple with the question of truth, and to ask whether *Aftershocks* can make any claim to being more 'true' than any other play. My response has always been that *Aftershocks* is a fabrication, just like any other drama spun from a writer's head. Perhaps it will seem like 'the' truth. But it was constructed from a particular process. It started with a terrible event which provoked the idea for a play and it was brought to life by a group of interested people who steered the project. It required research, taped interviews, transcription, culling, editing, a cut and paste, structuring, another cut and paste to generate a script. Then, turning a new corner, exploration by cast, director and crew, a new arrangement of the text and the usual elements of production. Finally there's the storytelling that takes place in performance.

I look at it this way: in a stage performance, the audience will perceive, in any one speech, three voices speaking in unison. First, the real person whose story is told; second the voice that emerged in interview (determined by the relationship across the microphone); and third, the voice of the actor, found through an exploration of text and history, but determined by a storyteller's commitment to entertain.

Each exploration by cast and crew, like an archaeological dig, is bound to make new discoveries. Some will seek out the people whose story is being told, thereby grounding a performance in what they know about personal circumstances, family, workmates and friends. Others will try to discover something of the dynamic of the taped interviews, for without this the passage of story from life to the stage remains mysterious. There's also a dramaturgical focus that will concentrate on language—sentence structure and speech patterns. The architect's plan of the old club, which maps the orderly configuration of concrete and steel that was destroyed in less than a minute, is, for almost everyone, buried treasure.

The stories could be told simply by reading them from a book, with no set, props, lights, or costume (indeed the very first presentation of the rough draft did this successfully). But it is better to own up to it as theatre, and in doing so obtain a balance between its initial simplicity and the heightened form of storytelling that will inevitably emerge from the discoveries made by each cast, director and crew.

FROM STAGE TO FILM

In the early 1990s Australian plays such as *The Sum of Us* (1993) and *Hotel Sorento* (1994) were becoming films. Film director Geoff Burton who had worked on such projects suggested that *Aftershocks* should follow suit. At almost the same moment, producer Kingston Anderson, who had been Director of the Hunter Valley Theatre Company, approached WCAC offering to raise funding for the film. Ultimately Julia Overton became the film's producer, with Newcastle cultural worker Julie Pavlou Kirri providing the all-important liaison between the film company and WCAC.[17]

Aftershocks, never a conventional play, was not likely to be a conventional film—neither in its style, nor its legal agreements over ownership. For a start, the production entity established to make the film was set up to include the WCAC as a company director, ensuring that a substantial proportion of the power over the film resided in Newcastle Trades Hall.

The progress from initial interviews to a play then a film, prompts many questions about control over stories originally told to researchers within the carefully negotiated and relatively 'safe' environment of the interview. This was heightened by the sometimes rapacious traditions of the film industry and by the power of the distributors, funding bodies, lawyers and underwriters who populate the scene. 'Try to get their stories for one dollar' was the first advice we received. But in the end, the deal over 'up front' payments and the distribution of 'back end' profits was structured to include the people whose stories were used and the researchers who conducted the original interviews. 'Christ, negotiating that will be a nightmare' was the advice. But it wasn't—it just took time and care. Perhaps the best protection against a loss of control came from the decision to maintain the 'verbatim' approach of the play. To pursue this on film helped guarantee that the stories were close to the way their owners told them.

Some assessors of the film were uncertain about what they held in their hands. Here was a script whose dialogue was made up of grabs taken from carefully transcribed interviews with real people, suggesting documentary. Yet the words were to be spoken by actors (talking straight to camera) and these speeches, embedded in imagery and music, were edited to work like drama. The film industry is notoriously uncomfortable with material that falls between documentary and drama and film financing is structured to discourage such projects. We had become used to calling the play 'documentary theatre', but for our film venture, we quickly abandoned the word 'documentary' and began to talk the thing up as drama—not least because in the world of film financing anything branded documentary is bound to attract meagre dollars. Ultimately it was SBS Television that backed the project through its production arm SBS Independent.[18]

The film differs from the play in several respects. It opens out certain elements of the storytelling through images that could never be conveyed through theatre staging. It reconstructs fragments of memory suggested by the storytellers—a water pipe that spurts, a dead body covered with coins, the fracturing of an office wall. Larger effects, apart from being too costly, were resisted as unnecessary distractions from the work we wanted audiences to undertake in their imaginations. The film does make use of television footage, archival sound tracks, and stills photography—much as any documentary film would intercut such elements with 'talking head' interviews. The play puts sixteen characters on stage, but there are only eleven in the film because the visual material effectively covers contextual material about Newcastle, the club and the wider devastation caused by the earthquake.[19]

Another obvious difference is that actors play only one character in the film, and the attempt to 'transform' actors into the real people is more complete. The transformation is aided by a costume and a set that speaks of their professional or personal life., So Lyn is in a park, the barmaids Kerry and Marg are in a pub, the Bingo caller Stan Gill is in his beach shack hideaway, and John Constable is in his edge-of-town house that seems never to be a home. No version of the play has ever tilted towards such naturalism, since there's too much advantage in a single symbolic stage setting.

The longest narrative arc in both the play and the film is the story of John Constable, the young cleaner who makes daring rescue after daring rescue. What differs is that on stage John's character remained in balance within an ensemble of storytellers. He's important but doesn't dominate. For film, always a blunter instrument than theatre, there is an increased focus on John's character. He becomes something of a screen hero, is more psychologically rounded than any other character, and proportionally occupies more screen time. The film successfully pulls us in alongside his point of view.[20]

THE CORE OF THE EARTHQUAKE

On 3 December 1998, Newcastle Workers Club hosted the premiere screening of the film, and many whose stories are told were there. Some of these people had not previously set foot in the new club, which had risen on the site where their friends and workmates had been trapped, disfigured or killed. After the screening they stood on stage receiving loud applause. The screening was important, too, for the forty or so Newcastle-based cultural workers who had contributed to the project over its ten year life.

The new club was declared open on 2 July 1992. It is garish and in some respects cold, with a Las Vegas feel that the old club had avoided. It has yet to make its own history. The old club, with its half century of social and left wing political activity that made it the centre of the Newcastle labour movement, is a hard act to follow. The new club seems to lack this sense of a protected home base. But the night of the screening did create a chance to celebrate and remember, and in some small way to help make the traditions of the place.

The *Aftershocks* stories, combined and presented as theatre or film, make up what might be termed an unofficial story or truth about the earthquake. Not the crudely distilled version of television news, not the legalese of the official inquiry, but something more closely resembling what people near the heart of the matter might want recorded as Australian history.

The end has remained the same throughout the entire process. From the moment we heard John Constable's interviews there was never a doubt that a particular fragment would be conclusive. He relates his dream:

JOHN: (JC79) And I dreamt that I'd found the core of the earthquake. It was in the basement of the Workers Club. What it was was just this deep hole. I'd got all the bosses together and I said, 'Listen, this is where the earthquake comes', and they've gone, 'Bull'. And I've gone, 'Shhh, you'll have to keep quiet. If you talk too loud it'll start an earthquake.' They've gone, 'John, John, we want you to prove it'. And I've started down into this hole, and it's rumbled [*making a rumbling sound*] everywhere, and I've just darted into this little tunnel I knew come up near the door, the Union Street door. And my girlfriend's there. And I've said, 'What are you doing here? You're not supposed to be here.' And anyway I've gotten her out. And that was it... I'd found the core of the quake... And I'd just left all the bosses in the middle of the Club and I'd escaped my own way.

Sydney
May 2001

NOTES

1. This introduction to the second edition updates and adapts material I have previously used in documenting the *Aftershocks* project. The early stages were described in '*Aftershocks*: Verbatim Theatre about the Newcastle Earthquarke, a work in progress', in the Oral History Association Journal, Number 13 1991. Program Notes written for the play's production by Belvoir Street Theatre in 1993 are another source. I wrote about the transfer from stage to screen in '*Aftershocks*: Local stories, National Culture' in Meanjin Volume 54 Number 3, 1995.
2. Critical reviews of *Aftershocks* have focussed on it as 'documentary theatre' chronicling a real and important Australian event, and have many times commented on the vernacular language. After the 1993 Belvoir Street production, Brian Hoad in the *Bulletin*, (August 3 1993) again gave attention to its language, and described *Aftershocks* as a 'play that redefines the essence of theatre' and a 'landmark in Australian theatre'. To the extent that awards measure 'value' and 'ownership', it is interesting that in 1999, ten years after the Newcastle earthquake, the film version of *Aftershocks* was honoured twice, once when the Australian Writers Guild awarded it Best Adaptation from a stage play to a telemovie, and again by being nominated for the NSW Premiers Literary Award. Previously, the play received the Newcastle Condor awards for its script and its direction, and following the 1993 Belvoir Street production, it was nominated by the Sydney Critics' Circle as one of the best plays of that year.
3. The best available reference which brings together the issues of copyright and moral rights is *Copyright and Community Arts* put out by the Australia Council and obtainable through the Council's Community Cultural Development Board. *Aftershocks* is a case study in this publication.
4. Bob Phillips' Workers Club History *The Red Inn*, published by the Club in 1998, contains the most readable story of the Newcastle earthquake, as well as many remarkable photographs of the disaster at the Club. It also includes further details of how and why the Workers Cultural Action Committee established and funded the *Aftershocks* project.

5. This outline of subjects and themes grew out of several meetings between the writer, the steering group, the research team, WCAC, and Club workers. It was formalised in a document simply titled 'First Ideas', which was put forward for comment about one month into the project.

6. See Derek Paget's article 'Verbatim Theatre: Oral History and Documentary Techniques' in *New Theatre Quarterly* Vol 3 No 12, November 1987.

7. *The Laramie Project* was developed by the Tectonic Theater Project of New York. It played at Belvoir Street Theatre with an Australian cast, directed by Kate Gaul in March and April 2001. One of its cast, Lynette Curran, acted in both the film and the Belvoir Street productions of *Aftershocks*.

8. These three plays, in 1988, 1989 and 1990 respectively, were part of an on-going program of community plays by the MRPG. *Murray River Story* (Writer in Residence Paul Brown) used the recollections and opinions of people along the Upper Murray as the basis of a play about river ecology and history. The show was performed by a cast of about 60, and took place on the river itself. *Promised Land* (Writer in Residence Sonia Sedmak) was based on the stories of post-World War II immigrants who were housed at the Bonegilla Migrant Hostel outside Wodonga. The play was performed on the Albury Railway station with a cast of about 50 people. The third piece, *Two Cities* (Writer in Residence Paul Brown) concerned the development of the Albury Wodonga Growth Centre since the early 1970s, and was based on stories and opinion from Albury Wodonga residents. Again a cast of about 50 took part, with about 100 others involved in research, writing and production workshops. The play was performed on Monument Hill overlooking the two cities.

9. Those interviewed by Bob Phillips were all staff of the Club who had been in the building at the time of the collapse. They were Howard Gibson, Lyn Brown, Bob and Fay Asquith, Stan Gill, John Constable, Wayne Dean, Kerry Ingram, Richard Britliff, and Terry Ware.

10. Of the people already interviewed by Bob Phillips (*see* note 9), only Terry Ware and Richard Britliff were not interviewed a second time during the main research phase one year after the quake. New

interviewees were Elaine Gibson (Club staff), Jennifer Mathews (ex-Club staff), Margaret Lowndes (nurse), Eddie Seymour (Club Board member), Julie Pavlou Kirri (WCAC Organiser), Jeannette McMahon (ABC radio journalist), Jack Onslow (Club founding member), Peter Barrack (Club President, Trades Hall), Maureen Molloy (Club staff), Melba Middleby (Club founding member, ex-Club Board), David Ross (Ecology Centre, Hunter community Forum), Nina Bailey (Club patron), Margaret Turnbull (ex Club staff), Mark Smallcome (Minister), Stefo Nantsou (WCAC, Theatre worker), Dianne Barrack (Plumbers Union).

11. At the time the play was developed, there were also a number of research studies underway in Newcastle, and some of these were used resource material for the project. For example, Ellen Jordan from the University of Newcastle's Sociology Department had conducted interviews with police, ambulance and media personnel. The principle line of enquiry was about who held authority on the day of the earthquake.

12. All interviews, on tape or in transcript form, are available through the WCAC, from Newcastle City Library, or from the NSW State Library. Other research material for the project included nineteen interviews not on tape with union leaders, health workers, theatre workers and other Newcastle residents. Local radio and TV stations also provided tapes of broadcasts on the day of the earthquake.

13. These are extracts from the second edition of the play, which now includes the original references to numbered tape transcripts from which the play was made. For example, 'MT4' at the start of a speech refers to the fourth grab of Marg Turnbull's interview.

14. This and following quotes are from a transcribed record of the audience discussion after the First Reading. This record is kept by the WCAC.

15. This second edition of the play script is the original production draft used by WCAC and the Hunter Valley Theatre Company. However this varies only slightly from the First Edition which provided the draft used for Belvoir Street Theatre's production in 1993.

16. Set designers of later productions also made good use of chairs as key set elements. Chairs feature heavily in the recollections of rescuers and victims and therefore in the stories used in *Aftershocks*, because

staff were setting out chairs for an event in the main auditorium at the time the earthquake struck. They were chaotically thrown about and splintered, and entangled several people.

17. I regard the collaborative working relationship with Jules Pavlou Kirri, Julia Overton, Kingston Anderson and Geoff Burton as the 'engine room' which drove the film project forward over four difficult years.

18. The film *Aftershocks* was made for around $400 000, which would be seen as prohibitive by most filmmakers for a feature length telemovie. SBS Television provided more than half this budget.

19. For anyone comparing the characters in the film and the play, the five characters who do not appear in the film are Julie, Stefo, Wayne, Melba and Jenny. The story of Jenny's rescue by John is retained, but told only through John's eyes.

20. The film script, which I took through nine drafts between 1994 and 1997, has not been published, but can be requested from Sydney-based agent RGM Associates.

Aftershocks was first presented by the Workers' Cultural Action Committee with the assistance of the Hunter Valley Theatre Company at the Newcastle Playhouse, Newcastle, on 12 November 1991 with the following cast:

HOWARD, WAYNE	David Yarrow
BOB, STAN, EDDIE	Paul Makeham
JOHN, STEFO	David Cameron
LYN, MELBA, JULIE	Kath Leahy
ELAINE, MARG, PATRON	Rebecca Brandon
KERRY, FAY, JENNY	Sue Porter

Writer-in-residence, Paul Brown
Directed by Brent McGregor and David Watt
Designed by the Company
Lighting by Peter Ross
Project Administration, Julie Pavlou Kirri, and David Owens

Newcastle Workers Cultural Action Committee

Writer in residence: Paul Brown
Researchers: Carol Myers, David Owens, David Watt, Julie Pavlou-Kirri, Carole Collett, Paul Makeham, Vanessa Hutchins, Bob Phillips.

THOSE WHOSE STORIES ARE TOLD

LYN BROWN, in her forties, supervising cleaner at the club, who has worked there since she was nineteen. Lyn was trapped for about forty minutes on a narrow ledge

JOHN CONSTABLE, early twenties. A cleaner under Lyn's supervision. John took part in a number of rescues, including Lyn's

KERRY INGRAM, mid thirties. Bar attendant. She assisted with first aid on the footpath

HOWARD GIBSON, forty. Cleaner and Bar worker. He was injured in the shoulder

ELAINE GIBSON, about forty. Works in the poker machine room. She was not on shift at the time of the quake, but became involved when Howard walked home injured

MARG TURNBULL, mid thirties, Kerry's mate. She worked in the poker machine area, and also assisted on the footpath

FAY ASQUITH, about fifty. Fay was working with the hoy, and helped evacuate the patrons

BOB ASQUITH, fifties. Maintenance worker at the club. Helped with the rescues inside the club

STAN GILL, about forty. The Bingo and Hoy caller at the club. Stan rode a floor down and was injured quite severely

EDDIE SEYMOUR, thirties. club Board member who was away in Perth when the quake struck

JENNY MATHEWS, about twenty. On work experience at the club. Knew John Constable from Stockton. Trapped by the leg and rescued by John

JULIE PAVLOU KIRRI, thirty. Trade Union artsworker who lives near the club

STEFO NANTSOU, thirty. Artsworker who lives near the club

WAYNE DEAN, late thirties. The club's Secretary Manager. Helped with rescues, evacuation.

A PATRON, in her sixties. A club patron who was trapped in the collapse

MELBA MIDDLEBY, founding member of the club

DOUBLING SUGGESTIONS, FOR A CAST OF SIX

LYN, MELBA, JULIE

ELAINE, MARG, PATRON

KERRY, FAY, JENNY

JOHN, STEFO

HOWARD, WAYNE

BOB, STAN, EDDIE

SETTING

The simplest possible. Perhaps six chairs, perhaps some writing on the back wall that reads as if it's a quote from an interview:

> 'December the twenty-eighth nineteen eighty-nine, at about ten twenty-seven, I can recall feeling a shudder in the building…'

or [as with the first production in Newcastle] a list of scenes on the back wall.

NOTES

Initials followed by numbers in the script (eg KI9, SG15) are reference numbers to the original transcripts. Two people (Diane Barrack and Jack Onslow) were interviewed but do not appear as characters. Their transcribed words are spoken by another character. In rare situations one character is given words taken from another character's interview. Fay and Bob are the only characters that were interviewed together.

Scenes often begin with an actor speaking the title, for example 'Lyn's Shoe'. This is one way for the actors to confirm that they are primarily storytellers rather than the characters themselves.

SCENES

ACT ONE

1:	Work Routines	KERRY, HOWARD, STAN, MARG, JOHN, LYN
2:	Lyn's shoe	LYN
3:	Collapse	ELAINE, HOWARD, BOB, KERRY, FAY
4:	Stan's Ride	STAN
5:	Trapped	JOHN, LYN
6:	Bicycle	STEFO
7:	First Aid	MARG, KERRY
8:	Poker Machine Room	BOB, JOHN, HOWARD
9:	Just Here to Play Hoy	THE PATRON
10:	Priorities	BOB, FAY, HOWARD, ELAINE
11:	Perfectly Still	LYN, JOHN
12:	I want to forget	STAN

ACT TWO

13:	Jump Club	MELBA, HOWARD, ELAINE, EDDIE, KERRY, STEFO
14:	Barriers	EDDIE, JULIE
15:	Service Industry	WAYNE, LYN, JOHN
16:	Adrenalin	KERRY, MARG
17:	Cellar Level	ELAINE, JOHN, BOB
18:	Jenny	JENNY, JOHN
19:	Homes	HOWARD, ELAINE, FAY, BOB, JOHN, LYN
20:	Marg's Car	MARG
21:	Requiem	EDDIE
22:	Ladder	JOHN, LYN
23:	Flowers on the Gate	KERRY, HOWARD, ELAINE, EDDIE, FAY, BOB, LYN, JENNY, JULIE
24:	Escape	JOHN

ACT ONE

SCENE ONE: WORK ROUTINES

KERRY, HOWARD, STAN, MARG, JOHN, LYN

Sounds of the Club (pokies, chatter, bar noise, etc.) can be heard as the audience and the actors enter. They fade out.

KERRY: (K19)You go in, you put your money in the till, you open the bar up, and then do the normal procedures. Stock the fridge if it needs stocking. You could be out the back for five minutes, or ten minutes, sorting out glasses and setting that up, and then you got nothing to do, and normally you go out for a walk around the poker machines, pick up any odd glasses that are out there, or go and pick up the change cups for the girls in the poker machine kiosk, and take that over, and have a quick yatter, and so forth, and do the normal things, chat up the regular drunks.

HOWARD: (HG13) On a Hoy day we organise everything downstairs. Occasionally when there's something on in the old auditorium, we shift the Hoy ladies over the other side 'cause the ladies don't like it either. They get very irate about being shifted around.

STAN: (SG15,18) Hoy is very similar to Bingo, but instead of using numbers you call the cards. In Hoy they got two boards, and they got the cards on 'em. Like aces and jacks. And I just flick the cards over, and I call the cards out, say, okay, 'Jack a Hearts, Jack a Hearts'. If they've got the Jack a Hearts on their board, they put a coin or something on it. And as soon as that board's filled up they yell out, and they're out. I enjoy doing the Bingos. Two fat ladies and one little duck, and two ducks, legs eleven, unlucky for some, key to the door, thirteen twenty-one, yeah. But the Hoy is a more popular game. See Bingo they get twenty games, Hoy they get sixty. For less money. They're only paying a dollar for two boards.

HOWARD: (HG13) If there's a concert on at night, all our blokes'll be pretty heavy into getting stores up into the main auditorium, and getting the whole place going. Up into the old section, in the old auditorium, and there's a lift that goes right up into the... services the bar, and also the kitchen above. There's all the ordering for the catering. The spirits, beer, and most other things. And it's comin' in all the time.

MARG: (MT38) Every day you just read the cancelled credits and the jackpot meter. Once a week you do a full read, which means every machine in the Club, which is about a hundred and ninety-five machines. They've all got six meters, and you read all six meters on every machine. Then it's all punched in a computer, and everything's balanced out, as to money and jackpots... whatever's paid out on jackpots, whatever's paid out cancelled credits, and it all balances. It's gotta balance. If it doesn't, you look for it.

KERRY: (KI30) It's only a job. I'm only a number there. I stand behind a bar, put up with obnoxious people. I do my job. I'm not dedicated to the place. No way. My family come first before that bloody place does.

Focus on JOHN *alone.*

JOHN: (JC36, 37, 38) The place was amazing. Just every nook and cranny. I've been in the roof, on the roof, underneath stages, above stages, up where the chandeliers are in the big auditorium. The place was so huge and the chandeliers up there were just massive. You had these big winches to wind 'em down and change light bulbs and clean 'em. Beside the stage was a fire exit, just a small little square and then they had the door there that led down. Down the basement itself is the door from the basement of Trades Hall. There's a door there and if you open up the door, it led straight to the cellar at the top. You know, where the stairs went down to your meeting rooms or whatever there was a door on your left... that led straight to the cellar. That's where all the grog was. That's why it's a steel door... Get the oxy gear out... [*Laughing*] Pouring down in the middle of winter, I was up on top of the roof with one of the other casuals. We were sitting there, full wet weathers, sitting on the roof doin' a tap dance to the people on the streets... *pouring* down rain, we had to go up and clean the gutterings, 'cause the guttering was getting blocked and making leaks into the Club, so we had to go up there and get all the stuff out of the gutterin'. While we were up there [*singing, laughing*] 'dah da dah da dah da dah', these people were looking up, gaping, 'wow'. Wearing the hat, full wet weather gear... it was great.

Focus on LYN *alone.*

LYN: (LB36) You had your special moments with a lot of the patrons... I'm sure a lot of them think of me as their daughter sometimes, or part of their family, because there's not just one of them... I've probably got dozens of them that will seek me out. I get their little Chrissie presents off them...

(LB38) I get up at four. Four a.m.. I don't do a lot before... because everyone is still asleep... just do a little bit of work out in the lounge room, where the children can't hear me, and my husband can't hear me... just tidying up, mainly. If they've left their dishes from the night before, I do those. I have breakfast, go in and have a shower, get dressed and go to work.

(LB13) We clean the mezzanine section first... everything, kitchen, bars, tables and ashtrays, carpets, toilets, and offices. Then move into the old auditorium, and then into the Meeting Place, the Blue Room. Then we finish off in the new auditorium, a full eight, eight and a half hour day, the usual routine.

(LB14) For a rock concert. We'd start in the new auditorium first, at two a.m.... Use garden rakes to rake up the cans, off the floor, we just rake them all up in piles, and pick them up, and I'm talking about sometimes... forty bags, you know, of cans, maybe more. And then we vacuum, then we wash the dance floor, a huge dance floor... quite a few hours. Because you're looking at mud.

(LB16) We constantly used to find pieces of underwear everywhere, I mean that was a constant day-to-day thing, but... just the underwear, you'd find it in the strangest of places, you know, probably just out on the deck, you know, draped over a chair, or under a chair, or something like that... and some'd be discreet, they'd go to the toilets, and leave them there.

(LB44) If I want to change anything, as a supervisor I virtually just do it myself. It's in place, and there's nothing they can say, once it's in place. And then I just go to Wayne, and I say, 'What do you think of this idea'... 'Yes, Lyn, that's a good idea', and I say, 'Great, it's done.'

JOHN *also into focus.*

JOHN: (JC35) Great boss, great boss to work for... oh yeah... best boss I've ever worked for and it's a woman... Yeah, Lyn's a top lady. She'd ask me to come in to do a cleaning shift in the morning: [*melodically*] 'No problem'. I'd get up for it 'no worries' 'cause I enjoyed doing it. Some'n different. So... she thought I was that good of a worker. I'd work for her anywhere, any job. If she was a boilermaker, I'd still work under her.

LYN: (LB26/27) He was like a son, John. He was probably one of my biggest... not problems, but I helped him, with his personal life... Particularly with training, because he came out of the bar, and into my section.

JOHN: (JC34) She had little finicky things on the roster. Like steam cleaning the floors, cleaning the windows, or do the light bulbs.

LYN: (LB26,27) My... my staff did everything. They knew I expected them to do their things right, but I was very very fair. Everything that had to be done in that club, my staff did.

◆ ◆ ◆ ◆ ◆

SCENE TWO: LYN'S SHOE

LYN

LYN: [*announcing the title*] 'Lyn's shoe'... (LB1,2,3,4) I've lost my shoe off my foot... I was just getting up off my chair. I was going to check my staff, because they'd been on their break, and we had a rock concert that night, and I'd been doing some rosters... and that's how I lost my shoe... It was only a flat shoe, so that's all the more amazing. Everything happened in a split second... Perhaps when I was sitting there... you've got your shoe sort of half on and half off type of thing… and… oh gee… like… the rumble came, the movement of the ground, and at that stage I was on my feet because the lights went out… and that virtually would have been my job to go and find out why they went out… not to fix it, but to find out what was going on… Something's falling off the roof. I get up from the desk, walk one step, and then the lights are out. One more step, and I see all the bricks come down… just at my doorway. And everything just keeps tumbling. The big unit, the air conditioning unit, comes off the roof… just sheers straight down in front, and everything just keeps on falling. I don't scream. And as quick as it starts it stops. And I sort of stop, and look around. I know every inch of that club, but I can't orientate myself. Just nothing left there. Just quietness, you know, really it's just so still. Then the alarms and the screaming…

SCENE THREE: COLLAPSE

ELAINE, HOWARD, BOB, KERRY, FAY

Focus on HOWARD *and* ELAINE *as a couple.*

ELAINE: 'Howard and Elaine's story'.

HOWARD: (HG19) Elaine and I used to run the pub. Back in the mid eighties, when the Workers Club purchased the Newcastle Hotel. Prior to that I was the Club's purchasing officer, and back when I first started in 1968, I was a poker machine mechanic. Currently I'm a cleaner. That's the position that suits me at this present point in time.

ELAINE: (EG27) Fifteen years ago we were both working at the Club. And we've both been divorced, and we've both got children from a previous marriage. And I was left with four little children. And Howard and I used to talk at the Club, but we were friends. Then when my little boy got very sick and I had to go down to Sydney… One time Howard came with me. And they weren't going to let my boy back out of hospital, and they were saying how are you going to cope with this back home, on your own. And Howard just said, 'She won't be on her own'. And that was it.

HOWARD: (HG16) I've been preoccupied with... mainly with family matters... family affairs... we've got a rather large family. We both have a family from those previous marriages, and ah, the offspring from both those marriages have been quite large. My wife does happen to be Catholic, but that's got nothing to do with the producing of offspring between us. So basically I'm a family man, I suppose.

ELAINE: (EG24) Five o'clock in the morning, and I was night work, the night before, so I was still in bed. Howard got up, had a little bit of breakfast, got dressed, and he always comes up and kisses me goodbye when he goes, and then he went to work, and that's... Walked to work, Howard walks to work. He's always early for work. Fifteen minutes early for work.

HOWARD *'goes to work'.*

HOWARD: (HG13,21) There was a normal Thursday crew. I was rearranging furniture in the main auditorium and setting up for a concert that was due that night... the chairs and so forth, tables and chairs. And Stan Gill approached me and was talking about the problem with the lights that he'd had down in the area where they play Hoy, and would I be able to go down and fix that light up. And at that time, that was the time when the earthquake actually hit... 'Kerry's Story'.

KERRY: (K11) I was in the Mezzanine Bar... first panel... first panel of the bar tap. So... and I just finished serving a customer... and put the milk back in the fridge, and... turned around, I just started to wipe the bar top over and all of a sudden there was this massive explosion. First I thought someone had been kicked out and they were real mean, and they'd come back and bombed the place.

HOWARD: (HG22,23) The walls were basically like flags in the wind, just flapping in the wind. Unbelievable that brick walls could do that. Those big chandeliers, that's what caught my eye, was the fact that the chandeliers were coming down. And I thought that must be... the whole mechanism must've shaken loose, because they were on hydraulic, sort of, wheels.

KERRY: (K12,13) The ceiling, it was… just like it was gradually crawling towards the bar the way it was coming down and … then the first thing I saw that did come away was the back wall… and that's when the whole roof just kept coming and coming. The concrete slab of the floor above was coming down. I was thrown from the beer panel, and I hit the fridge. I must have lost my footage and I fell to the floor… And the beer panel closed up behind me and all I could remember… My husband John's a miner's deputy… when there's a mine explo… a mine cave-in, you, you stay low and you grab hold of something because the air goes this way and there's nowhere for the air to go. So I was just hanging onto the rods, and saying a few prayers…

Focus on BOB *and* FAY *as a couple.*

BOB: 'Fay and Bob's story'.

FAY: (FA/BA27) The day the earthquake struck, we'd done the normal things. Got the boards out and got set up for the Hoy. And the ladies started to come in. It was a bus strike and a lot of 'em got in early… And just set everything up, and I was talking to one of the other girls I work with, and I said I'm just going downstairs for a minute. That was about twenty-seven minutes past.

BOB: (FA/BA27) 'Cause you had to get a membership application form for your nephew.

FAY: (FA/BA27) I'd been gonna get it for weeks and weeks, and I forgot. And this particular day I said I'm just going down to get it… And as I went to walk away, everything started to shake and shudder. I'll never forget the noise. And the timbers and that coming down.

BOB: (FA/BA27) The death of a building.

FAY: (FA/BA27) It was like a building in pain, like screeching, and groaning… and then total silence, as everything just settled. It came slowly. It was… it was agonising. It was a terrible feeling.

BOB: (FA/BA27)There was so much RS… steel RSJs through the place, up in the ceiling of the auditorium… the timber, I mean there musta been hundreds of thousands of dollars worth of timber…

FAY: (FA/BA27) Beautiful.

BOB: (FA/BA27) It was all oregon. Beams like this.

FAY: So you could imagine the noise of that. And all the cement, just falling. I could imagine what it'd be like in a war zone.

BOB: No, you couldn't.

FAY: No, but that would be a little part of it, say, it'd be horrific to be in a war zone type of thing.

Focus on HOWARD *and* ELAINE.

HOWARD: (HG25) There were pieces of concrete that would've fallen on me. And some did actually fall on me, but the... but I was cushioned because of the... of the fibrous plaster tiles that were ceiling material had fallen onto me first. And then the slabs of concrete then fell on top of the fibrous plaster.

ELAINE: (EG22) When it hit him, he was laying on the ground, and he was winded. The wind had gone out of him and he couldn't breathe. And he said he really thought he was going to die. He was waiting for concrete slabs to hit him on the head. He couldn't breathe. He was... He thought this is it. And... nothing hit him on the head. And he got his wind back. It was actually chairs that saved him, because the concrete slabs had rested on the chairs, and didn't fall on top of him, on his head. It fell up to here [*indicating chest level*] and didn't fall on this part.

She indicates her head.

HOWARD: (HG26,27) Then there was no more vibration and no more concrete... When the earthquake hit, Stan went west, and I went east. I was talking to him, right at the critical moment. He said in pretty clear verbiage: 'What the fuck was that?' And I responded to that in similar mode, and I said... 'I don't know'. And just by sheer luck, by, I don't think it was instinct or anything else, just by sheer luck, he went west, and I went east. Stan ran towards the western side of the Club, and as the building collapsed, each floor went down, the dance floor went down with it. The dance floor was, instead of being flat, was out, pointing down like a slippery-dip. All went down and along with it went Stan, on a slippery-dip type thing.

◆ ◆ ◆ ◆ ◆

SCENE FOUR: STAN'S RIDE

STAN

STAN: 'Stan's ride'… (SG30) I rode the floor down. And as the concrete hit the floor [*clapping his hands*], I've sorta BANG with the concrete floor, and BANG up again, and I'd say what's happened is the chairs've come underneath, 'cause I ended up all tangled up in chairs, and me arms up in the air and stuff like that.

(SG3) Whereas just before that, okay no worries, Howard Gibson and me, we yak yak yak… about these globes that needed replacin'… The old ducks, they can't see… so you know what Howard's like. Well Howard always does those things for me, and if I ask him, then sorta, they're done straight away.

(SG21) I remember I looked at him, while it was going on, we could hear this massive roar, this sorta, huge, like a bloody underground train coming… and then we stopped talking… There was three big, long, slow waves, and the whole floor just collapsed, and he musta seen it and bolted for an opening. Yeah, Howard went east, and I went west.

(SG25) I never been close to death… I knew I was… the first thing that struck me, as the floor started to give way, and I went down with it, the first thing that hit my mind was, hello I'm dead.

(SG24) I sorta looked up. Everything was coming down. Then it gave this great big puff! Like the air and everything, big puff of wind, and the whole… big dust thing went straight up in the air, went straight back up. And when everything sorta got quiet, that's when they all started screaming, I could hear all the people screaming. The ones who were actually trapped, y'know.

(SG28) All the bloody sound gear was lying everywhere. I could see all these wires hanging down and apparently I started yelling out. I don't remember doin' it, but I was, y'know… 'Fer Chrissakes, will somebody get me out of this fuckin joint'.

He laughs.

(SG7) I just heard someone yell out, 'Get jacks, get jackhammers, get the ambulance, get the police, get the lot', words to that effect. I wouldn't have recognised the voice. 'Mate, I've done something to me back', I said, 'I don't care how much you hurt me, but for Chrissake get me out of these chairs.'

(SG23) And the most vivid thing I remember about it... I couldn't move 'cause me back was too sore... I ripped me shoes off, thinking that might let me get out of the chairs a little bit better, and what terrified me the most was when I looked up and the bloody dance floor was still there. How, I dunno why. Like all around the whole dance floor, everything just come down. You got this massive... you been to the main... you been up in the main auditorium...? Well, that dance floor's still there. I dunno how it stayed there, but that dance floor was actually still hanging there.

◆ ◆ ◆ ◆ ◆

SCENE FIVE: TRAPPED

JOHN, LYN

JOHN: (JC39) Lyn had me in at six-thirty that morning. It was a Hoy morning, so we had all downstairs to clean, and then upstairs to the old auditorium to set it up before nine-thirty, before they all... and I mean it was unreal, like a herd of sheep. Nine-thirty came and there'd be a barrage of old pensioners up the stairs, searching out a table you know, flying. [*He makes a noise like he's trying to avoid being knocked to the ground.*] That's what they were like though... *up* the stairs they just ran . Like you'd watch 'em go *down* the stairs after, they'd be hobbling and holding onto the side of the rail and that sort of stuff... and running *up* the stairs hell for leather.

(JC40,42,43) Anyway, me and Greg, who's turned religious, oh I'd say about nine months before or something... he was right into it at that time... he was sort of trying to push it onto people and, this is an omen for ya [*laughing*] ... that morning he's telling me I'm very biblically minded and all that sort of stuff, and I don't mind having a yak about the Bible, it's pretty intriguing, but I tell him it'd take tidal waves, floods... earthquakes... it'd take all that before I went to church with him...Thank God Lyn sent us down the Union

Street door. I'd be in the middle of it if she didn't. [*Mimicking Lyn's firm voice*] 'Do the windows and clean the lights, the big round ball lights.' And I said, 'Leave it out, Greg can do that by himself… How about I vacuum the new auditorium?' 'Cause the new auditorium needed a vac. It was pretty filthy. 'I'll just vacuum the auditorium.' 'No, go down'… 'Come on', I said, 'You don't need two people doin' that.'…'Go down and do it.'… [*Laughing*] Greg's down on the ground, and I'm there up this big ladder, A-frame, a pretty tall ladder, I'm up top of that, big glass ball in my hand. All of a sudden rumble rumble, boom… Mid-air mate, and I'm running. Hit the ground. [*He makes a noise like a car's wheels taking up*.] Straight out the door, don't break the ball. Put it back inside the door. Explosion, BHP, that sort of thing, gas, or something like that? Anyway, I've just bolted out the door…

(JC2) And I turn around and look back at the Club, and my jaw drops in unbelief you know. I can't believe what had happened, and I've gone: 'Ah, no'. So I, I run, I run back in there fast as I can.

(JC44) All the pensioners are comin' out that door… I'm sorta pushing my way, 'Excuse me, excuse me', and they're all flat out *down* the stairs like they were goin *up* the stairs. [*Laughing*] They don't care about their purses or nothin'.

(JC3) And I've just bolted straight to the auditorium, 'cause you can see that the roof'd collapsed in the auditorium, and Howard's come out and Howard looks shook, Howard Gibson, Howard's shook right up… and he's goin', 'What the fuck happened, what's goin' on?' And all he could see was dust and white light… just the dust coming out. And I said, 'Is there anyone else in there?' And Howard's goin', 'Stan's in there somewhere. Stan's in there somewhere.' And I'm sort of, 'Oh no', and I've ran in there as fast as I could… The balcony's just slumped right down. Dropped within four feet of the floor. I'm sittin' there crawling underneath, shoutin', 'Stan, Stan', shoutin' out, 'Stan'. I'm just looking around and I thought, [*with a small laugh*] 'Naaaa'.

(JC46,47) Then I think, 'Where's Lyn'. And her office is right up the top, right *near* the west wall, and everyone's saying, 'We don't know, we haven't seen her, we don't know what's happened', and I've gone, 'Ah no'.

Focus on LYN *trapped.*

LYN: (LB3) My desk was still standing there. And right next to me right shoulder, 'cause my office is so very small, the sides of the wall right next to me, opened up… There are cracks, two and three feet wide, and it is virtually just hanging. And the roof is… what's left of the roof is just sort of, still hanging down there too. 'The rest of it's gotta come down. It's just gotta keep coming, and nothing can keep it up there.'… I was frightened to move actually… 'Well it can't stay up any longer… It's going to come down, and the rest of the office has gotta come with it, 'cause it was just so attached to it.' So I just tried to stand as still as I could… You know, you talk about your knees shaking, and you know… I mean mine were, and at first really quite uncontrollable. They just felt as if you were going like that, but… yes I tried to stand as still as possible. And 'round me the Club is gone. I can see as far as Hamilton, straight down King Street without moving me head. And up to Bull Street… There's just nothing.

◆ ◆ ◆ ◆ ◆

SCENE SIX: BICYCLE

STEFO

STEFO: (SN1) As soon as it struck, I got on the bike, took a ride down Tudor Street, and as I got closer to Beaumont Street it was obvious that something very big had happened. Saw the damage at the chemist, and the toy shop, saw the bricks on top of people in the Kent Hotel. Had a look at the house where I used to live, and a whole wall had come away, so I was glad I wasn't living there anymore.

(SN10) I saw me parents' place was fucked… that was it, and I thought… oarrgh… that's my parents' life savings all up in smoke there… it's gone. There's nothing you could do, and I didn't want to be in the way.

(SN3) From there I got straight up town, and rode up Hunter Street. Saw the damage along Hunter Street. Headed up to the east end, to see me… two people who lived up there in terraces

David Cameron as Stefo in the 1991 WCAC production. (Photo: David Owens, WCAC.)

that I thought'd be down for sure. They weren't. They were safe. Fine. Check ya. Didn't wanta hang around too much. Headed straight back up King Street… And this is all within about fifteen minutes after it happened… And it was great. I've gotta be honest it was very exciting. It was very exciting… Saw the shit up King Street. That was all a mess. Didn't see anyone hurt yet. Got to the Workers Club, and that's when… that's where all the pandemonium…

(SN4) I mean, there was the Workers Club which had literally whole groups of people stunned, in the way, and shouting at each other.

(SN12) All these emergency workers, police and ambulance people shouting and screaming at each other, and shouting and screaming at people… definitely not handling it… The shock on everyone's face… like you know, the look on everyone's face of disbelief, and incomprehen… incomprehensible nature of the whole thing. People, you know, sort of still shaking.

(SN7) And there was that sorta sense of people at a car accident, you know, like you see a car accident, you hang around and you watch what'll happen. It was a huge stack, just like any other event, only it just happened to be an earthquake and lots of people died. So you're gonna hang around, and you're gonna watch, and you're gonna get in the way. And you'll try and get as close as possible.

SCENE SEVEN: FIRST AID

MARG, KERRY

KERRY: (MT30) We're just lining people up, like you see in a war zone, you know… all on the median strip. In sections, as to who is hurt more than others.

MARG: (MT9) We know an awful lot of the people that we're getting out, and the people that are so badly hurt, we just know them.

KERRY: (K14) One of them is out to it. Get her on her side, coma position, can't get her teeth out… and this other chappy comes up and he says, 'Look I'm an ex-ambulance man'. So he gets her bottom teeth out.

MARG: (MT7) The girls from the kitchen are hurt, 'cause everything just flew off the stove all over them. A few of them are covered in boiling water, and whatever.

(MT18) And traffic is still on King Street. Traffic is still flowing and we're carrying people across the streets, dodging cars… [*Laughing*] It's incredible. They don't even know there's been an earthquake… they just don't know what's happened.

KERRY: (MT30) There's no ambulances, and we're flagging down cars on the street… to take people to hospital. And Wayne's asked for anybody… any, any staff that got knowledge of first aid, can they give a hand… and we're doing tourniquets to our clientele that were in there and just stopping the… you know, stopping the bleeding…

MARG: (MT4) We're just trying to stop bleeding with our bare hands, type of thing… which is, you know, friggin' difficult.

Sue Porter as Kerry and Rebecca Brandon as Marg in the 1991 WCAC production. (Photo: David Owens, WCAC)

KERRY: (MT10) One lady that has a cut, I'm not exactly sure where it is, somewhere down between her fingers, and it's cut an artery or a vein or something, and every time her heart pumps, it's just pumping out. And we're actually holding her hand, squeezing it with our fingers, trying to stop her bleeding to death in front of us.

MARG: (MT10) And all she's worried about is her husband. She keeps saying that her husband was sitting in the car in the carpark. We've got no way of knowing whether he is or not. But we're holding her hand so tightly to try and stop this bleeding, the ring on her finger is cutting into her finger where we're squeezing it.

KERRY: (MT11) She just keeps saying, 'Let it go, let it go'. But we can't. If we let it go she'll bleed to death in front of us.

MARG: (MT10) My uniform is all covered in blood.

SCENE EIGHT: POKER MACHINE ROOM

JOHN, HOWARD, BOB

HOWARD: (HG26) Inside it was dark… 'cause the power was gone.

BOB: (BA29) Where I was stuck it was like being inside a cow. Couldn't see anything. I was lucky I'd opened the doors. If I hadn't had the doors open, I'd have been stuck in the lift.

HOWARD: (HG26) And I was lucky, my arms were still free. I could dig my way out from where I was stuck, along with the… with the close aid of two girls who I work with.

BOB: (BA30) I was confronted with all these mounds of chairs and tables that were stacked in this room. I'm fairly cool in that sorta situation… I'm still alive sorta thing… so, I knew where the door was. I been there for twenty-five years. I knew exactly where the door was… So I climbed over the chairs and… took me a coupla minutes, and I finally got out… I run down the stairs.

JOHN: (JC48) I go up the fire exit, down into the pokie area, past the Bistro, up the back stairs and there's two lots of fire stairs and I think, 'Oh, I'll go to Lyn's office that way'. Anyway, I've got to the down stairs to the pokies, just looked, [*a slow gasp*] 'Ahhhh'.

HOWARD: (HG4) We reached the kiosk where they served the poker machine change, to find nothing but rubble.

JOHN: (JC5) Here's the twenty-cent carousel, then your ten-cent machines across there, and there's more ten-cents there. Well the crack came along here, so you lost the twenty-cent carousel there, half the ten-cent…

BOB: (BA30) There was a ten-cent line that went across… half of them had gone.

HOWARD: (JC5) And then you had your five-cent there and there, and another twenty-cent carousel there… All that had gone straight through.

JOHN: (JC48,49) And I've just bolted *flat out* through all these people, because there are people screaming their heads off. This wire is hanging down and *whooppee* straight off a my feet, splatt, back up again, get up, and first thing I hear is this lady: [*in a high pitched voice*] 'Get this fucking thing off me'. She's swearing her head off, swearin' her head off.

BOB: (BA32) The next thing there was firemen coming up the stairs. They were the first there as far as I was concerned. The Cooks Hill Fire Brigade. And we could hear people screaming, and we were tryna pull stuff off them.

JOHN: (JC52) There are just poker machines everywhere. I'm just sitting there, picking 'em up, rolling 'em and this other guy beside me, he's only a job experience person. Ah the strength of that guy is great... blows me away. He's picking 'em up, pulling them over his shoulder. [*Laughing*] I'm lifting 'em and moving 'em, and he's just picking 'em over his shoulder and just throwing 'em.

BOB: (BA32) When they got money in them, they're heavy bastards. We were just pickin them up as if they were nothin'. I couldn't believe it. It was bloody terrible.

HOWARD: (HG32) They were trying to lift a very heavy piece of building material off somebody, and I said, 'Well I'll give you a hand', and I realised then I couldn't lift anything, because of the problems I had. So after a few minutes I think I just made my way onto the street.

HOWARD *goes out of focus.*

JOHN: (JC53) There's a couple of ladies, we just clear 'em totally of any weight of the poker machines and anything like that and just leave 'em and I'm sayin', 'Listen, we don't know what's wrong with ya, so we'll just leave you here and... yeah, a doctor and that will be here soon, so just lay down and try and stay calm'. And caressing 'em and stuff like that.

BOB: (BA32) And all the electric power cables are hanging down. And I thought gees I've just survived this and now I'm going to get electrocuted. You know we're tryna drag stuff off people, and I'm singin' out, 'Don't touch any of the bloody power lines, for chrissake. Yer gonna get electrocuted...'

JOHN: (JC6) I could see an arm sticking out from that side. So I've come around this side, and the guy had his legs pinned...

BOB: (BA30) I'd say he'd been sitting there playing the poker machines and it's cracked right under his feet. And what he's done, he's reached out and grabbed the poker machine. His legs have gone over the edge and the roof, which is the new auditorium floor, has just gone bang [*slapping his hands*] ... pinned his legs.

JOHN: (JC6) And I talk to this guy and he's gone, 'Ah mate, don't worry

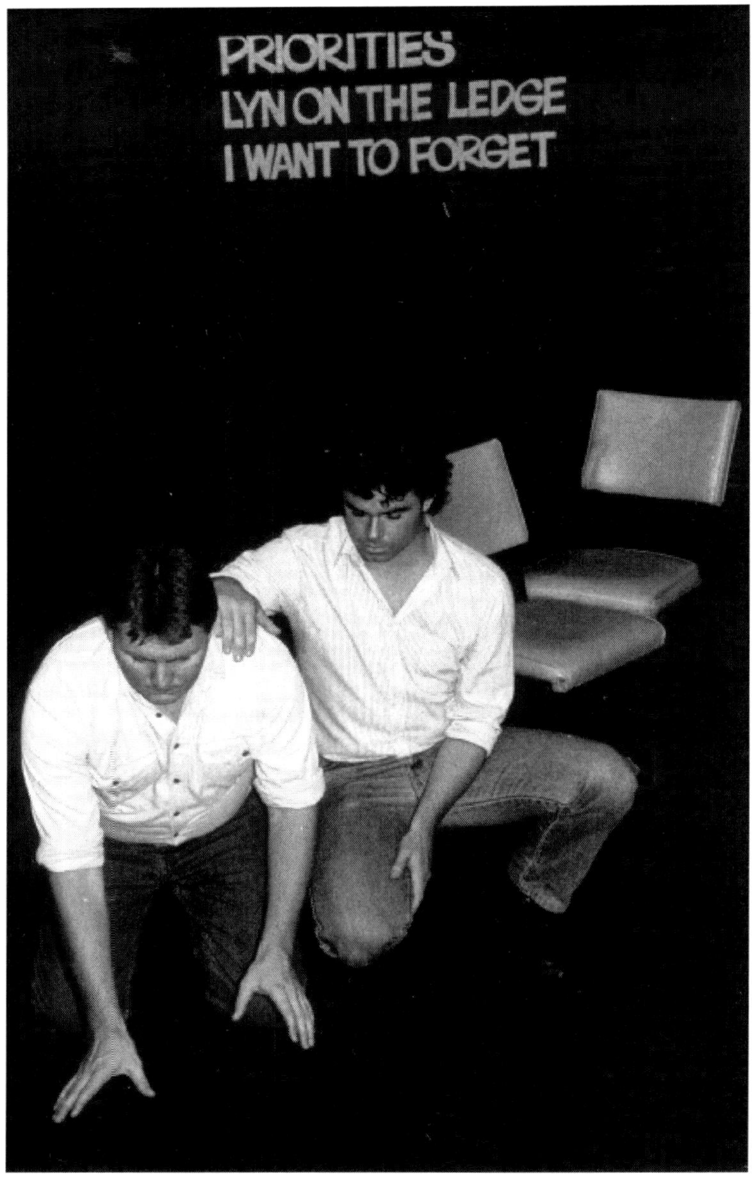

David Cameron as John and Paul Makeham as Bob in the 1991 WCAC production. (Photo: David Owens, WCAC)

about me. I'm cool, you know.' And his leg's bleeding like anything and… 'Ah noooo!'… He said, 'Go and help the rest of the people'. I said, 'Sure mate. Hey listen, we'll try and give you a hand.' He said, 'Naaa. I'll wait for the paros', and all that sort of stuff. Cool as a cucumber, no stress at all, no freakin' out.

BOB: (BA30) The roof of the kiosk had just collapsed into rubble and there was kiosk ladies in there, and we didn't know if any of 'em had gotten out or anything.

JOHN: (JC54) Someone has seen one of the striped shirts and I've freaked out a bit… I was sittin' there, 'Oh shit there's fuckin' kiosk staff in there. I was shakin' like anything and I was sittin' there pulling the coins and notes and rubble, you name it, wood, glass, everything, trying to find someone else.

(JC6) And I've gone, 'Oh, no'.

BOB: (BA30) She was covered in dirt and dust. You could see her uniform, but you couldn't tell who it was.

JOHN: (JC6) And there's hot water spl… keeps splashing in her face, 'cause there is a pipe runnin' across the top that has burst, you know… and anyway, I… ar… I'm just… ar… there's… ar… Bob he's beside me sayin', 'Calm down and watch the wires, John, they… they could be live.'… I know they aren't live, because all the lights have gone out, and I'm just sort of shoving all the wires, all the building materials and bricks, and stuff like that… Then I get to her, she's got from top to bottom, just money, all dollar coins, just stuff like that all over 'er… And I'm sittin' there wipin' it all off…

(JC54) Yeah, and… yeah, and I've seen her and I've thought, 'Oh no'. Anyway I've just put me hand straight up underneath her throat, to see if she has a pulse, and I'm that scared, my pulse is overriding, and I know I'm feelin' me own pulse… And I'm sayin', 'Yeah, she's alive, she's alive'. The doctors have come over and done the same thing. 'I don't think so.' Anyway, he's ripped her chest open, he's put his finger on it and he's sayin', 'No, sorry mate'. He says, 'Come and give me a hand over here', and I'm sayin', 'No, fuck off'. I just sit there, clear her right out, pulled her out, pulled her aside.

(JC7) And we've lain her down on the side of the poker machines, and one of the firemen puts a blanket over the top of her.

BOB: (BA32) And one of the rescue workers said, 'Oh, we're not worried about the dead ones, we're worried about the live ones, get them out first'.

SCENE NINE: JUST HERE TO PLAY HOY

THE PATRON

PATRON: (NB2) I only had about a ten-inch square to breathe in, and I had to keep my hands up, pushing against the piece of poker machine laying ahead of me, to try and keep it from coming down. And a doctor came, and I was fast running out of oxygen, but he dug a hole at the side of me, and he passed me an oxygen mask and told me how to put it on, and then he gave me a needle, and then all I could think of was, 'Wriggle my toes'. And I wriggled my toes, and I thought, 'While I've got toes I've got feet, and while I've got feet I've got legs'. And I could hear them all talking about aftershocks… And they ordered the rescuers out… They ordered them out, as they are expecting an aftershock, and I said, 'Please don't leave me'. And they said, 'We won't leave you'. And they didn't leave me. They disobeyed their order. They didn't leave me… And all I could hear was something saying to me, 'Don't panic. Don't panic and you'll be all right. You'll be all right.' And I just clung to that.

(NB8) When they started to lift the poker machines off me, of course, everything started to fall. And they stopped, and that was when they pulled me up. They were hoping to get the stuff off the top of me, to lift me up that way. Instead of that they had to come 'round and get me under the armpits, and pull me up through this little space. I lost all muscle on both… practically all the muscle off my… both legs, as they pulled me up through this little square… that was the only way they could get me out. And… I had a… they got me out that way. And my husband… I don't know who… they told me that I was just a mass of black and blue, and very swollen as they got me out. And later when they gave my husband back the clothes, the… the flesh was still in the pantyhose…

Lynette Curran as Melba Middleby in the 1993 Belvoir Street production. (Photo: Paul Wright)

(NB1) When it first struck, the lights went out, and I was just pushed around like a rag doll, 'til I came to rest… I'd had a few five cents in my purse, so I thought, here goes, I'll go down to the five-cent machines and put some in… and I think I only put about three… I was there a little bit early because the buses were on strike… my husband took me in… I'd just come in to play Hoy at the Workers Club.

◆◆◆◆◆

SCENE TEN: PRIORITIES

FAY *and* BOB, HOWARD *and* ELAINE

Focus on FAY *and* BOB *as a couple.*

FAY: (FA/BA20) They were all in there playing Hoy. My mum was in there. And two minutes before the earthquake struck, I'd just spoken to Stan Gill as he walked past, and I said, 'You have a nice Christmas?' And he sorta give me a grin and went, and he said, 'Just watch those elastic bands on the Hoy boards, they cost you a cent each', he was sayin' to the ladies, havin' a joke with 'em.

(FA/BA11) When it all collapsed, you didn't realise what it was. You thought they'd dropped the atomic bomb, that's what you thought…

BOB: Oh, they finally gone mad and done it.

FAY: (FA/BA27) We helped everybody get out of the auditorium, and everybody just went outside, just left everything. Maybe the old part was gunna go… 'Get out, everybody get out.' So they were quite orderly going out, and we got 'em all out, and we said, 'Leave everything. Just go.' And when we went outside, we could see all the other buildings, all the devastation.

BOB: And then you thought, '*Mum's* in there'.

FAY: And I rushed in, and I'm singing out, 'Mum, where are you?', 'cause it was all dark, y'know. I'm singing out, 'Mum', and one of the ladies said, 'She's under a table'.

BOB: Your mother was all right. She's under the bloody table.

FAY: (FA/BA9,11) My mum knew what it was. She said, 'I knew it was an earthquake'. That's why she got under the table…

BOB: And you thought I was down under it all.

FAY: I started to shake, and I started to cry… One lady asked me…

BOB: This is a classic.

FAY: I was runnin' down the street lookin' for Bob and I'm cryin' and just about hysterical and she's… she pulled me up and said, 'Fay'. I said, 'Yes'. And she said, 'Do we get our dollar back for our boards?'

BOB: She's worried about her dollar.

FAY: 'Oh shit. Don't worry me,' I said, 'I couldn't care less about your money.'

Focus on ELAINE *and* HOWARD.

ELAINE: (EG19) My friend, Dianne, said she'd driven from home to Darby Street, and this woman was out on the street looking very shocked, and Dianne said, 'What's happened?' and this woman said, 'I think there's been an earthquake', and Dianne really laughed.

She said, 'Oh no, not in Newcastle', and kept driving… Thought it was a joke.

(DB3) And she walked into the Trades Hall office, and saw all the things… books and papers were all over the floor, and she'd thought, 'Oh… what's going on here?' And it didn't really hit her until she walked out of the back door of the Trades Hall, and there was the Club, all just crumbling down, and rescue men running 'round everywhere.

HOWARD: (HG33) It's only when I reached the footpath that I sort of… the… the gravity of the whole thing, emerged.

(HG34) I realised Christ, if it's done this to the Workers Club, I live in Parry Street, within less than a kilometre from the Club, in an old terrace place. I thought well, jeez. I knew my wife and some of my family were there. I thought well, I better get back around there. My wife could be under a pile of rubbish, and rubble. So I hot-footed it home.

(HG35) I looked up Laman Street… that seemed to cop… must have been one of the highs in the earthquake configuration. And… so I picked up speed. And on the way home someone… people were out the front, and one woman said to me, she said that she was a nurse, just by comment, just happened to coincide. So I said, 'Well get yourself 'round to the Workers Club. They need you 'round there.' So she took off to the Workers Club. And I was home within a few minutes of that.

ELAINE: (EG25) We ran outside the house… 'Oh no, it wasn't an earthquake.' And then when we found out it was, I thought, 'Oh we've had an earthquake. Howard'll be coming 'round the corner any minute to see if we're okay.' And just as I'm thinking that, Howard's coming 'round the corner, and I'm sort of waving to say, 'We're okay. We're okay.'… And I suddenly looked at him, and he was dreadful. He was in a state of shock. He couldn't breathe. He didn't have his arm in his… in his shirt. His shirt arm was out there, I s'pose he was like this. [*She demonstrates an awkward leaning position.*] His uniform was all white, it was torn, it was hanging out of his pants, and he was just bent over like this. And that's when I knew he was hurt. I just saw his face. And he said, 'The Club's gone'. He said, 'There's dead people', and he started to cry. He

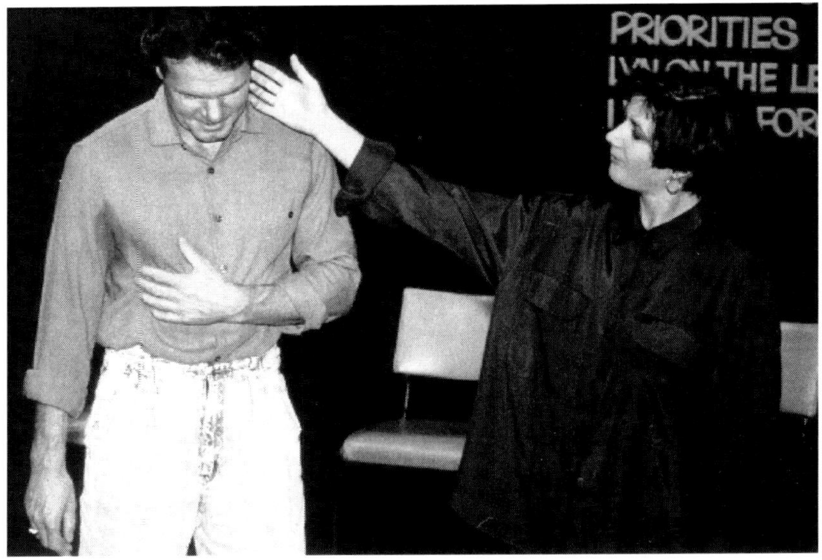

David Yarrow as Howard and Rebecca Brandon as Elaine in the 1991 WCAC production. (Photo: David Owens, WCAC)

wasn't worried about himself. He was just… and then after a while he kept on saying, 'I couldn't do anything'. He couldn't do anything. He couldn't lift, couldn't… 'cause with his ribs, tha… that's the part that upset him.

HOWARD: (EG3) And Elaine said, 'What about the girls in the kiosk?' 'cause that's where she works, and I said, 'They're digging them out'.

ELAINE: Oh, and I just… I sort of just ran, down to the Club.

HOWARD: And so I followed her, back down to the Club.

ELAINE: (EG4,6) I saw something on TV and you saw where they were digging the babies out, you know of that hotel in Mexico. And I pictured myself… nobody else being there… and I just thought I was gonna run down and dig people out. As soon as I turned Union Street, into King Street, there was a dead person laying in the gutter. It had a sheet over it, but there was a dead person laying there. It was like… stepping into your TV… to see something in Beirut or somewhere. It was just unrealistic.

HOWARD: (HG37) Outside the Club, I realised that no way would you push yourself forward with the gravity of people… were absolutely tied up with major death and carnage… I never got attended to but that doesn't matter. It didn't really matter much.

ELAINE: (EG9) Some TV people noticed Howard, while he was looking for medical attention. They said, 'Do you work here?' And Howard said, 'Yes'. And with that, they all came to him with microphones, and everything. And Howard was still in shock. He was going like this.

The storyteller shows how HOWARD *supported his right side with his arm.*

And that's how he got onto the news, that night. Howard was on TV.

◆ ◆ ◆ ◆ ◆

SCENE ELEVEN: PERFECTLY STILL

JOHN, LYN

JOHN: (JC8) All of a sudden I've gone, 'Oh Lyn'. [*Laughing at himself*] And I've gone, 'Oh no, that's right, I was goin for *Lyn*'.

LYN: (LB5) I don't know how long I was trapped there for, before I seen some workmen. And the rescue worker come around, the Police Rescue worker, and he looked up and seen me, you know, and… he said to me, 'Just don't move, lady, not even a centimetre'. And I said, 'This roof's…' I said, 'The rest of it's gonna come down, isn't it?' And… he said, 'Just stand still, perfectly still'. I don't know, they went away. The workmen went away, and I think that's when I felt panic. When there was no one there.

JOHN: [*calling*] Lyn!

SCENE TWELVE: I WANT TO FORGET

STAN GILL

STAN: (SG32) The stretcher broke in half. There shoulda been say six carrying it, and the bloody stretcher… Actually that's in the record book… It's got me name in it… 'A big man, as we were carrying him out, the stretcher broke, and he screamed out in pain.' I don't remember that. And what they done then, they got a table like this, a beer table, a long one, and they just laid me on the table and said hang on to the sides and they picked me up and carried me, put me in the garage at the… the Water Board garage. Even then I said, 'What happened?' 'Oh there's been a bloody earthquake that's come all the way from Sydney.' I knew nothing about an earthquake. I was in there about half an hour… I had to wait for the spinal ambulance. They had to have all the gear.

(SG38) All the interviewers or that sorta stuff, the TV. They haunted the bloody hospital. They drove everybody bloody mad. In the end the nurse come around… 'Would you like an interview?' I said, 'No, I don't want one, thanks'. All I wanted was me hair washed and they wouldn't wash me hair. I dunno why…

(SG39) I still get 'em now. I get the real bad sniffs and the blinks, y'know. I blink like that. And that's why I went to the… after about two months I made an appointment to see this psychologist. Well I had three months with the psychologist.

(SG12) *He laughs.*

I was… I'm a fisherman, mate. And a surfer. A surfer and a bloody fisherman. I love me old beach fishing and that sort of stuff. I do a lot of beach fishin' at Dixon Park, and Bar Beach… I go on holidays up Stockton Beach for about three weeks every year… Me mate's got a hut up there, a shack. We have a lovely week's seven or eight days' holiday on Stocko Beach.

(SG36) Now I can't jog, or I can't run. Say I can turn the water on in a shower or in a bath, and it can be hot, and I don't feel it. I don't feel it straightaway. I can't lay on the sand. I can sit on the sand, but if I lay on the sand, I get a funny neck. I got a real kinky sort of neck. So what I do now if I go to the beach, I just dig a great big hole out and sit in it like a little chair, y'know, like a little bloody chair on the sand.

(SG35) I had a look at the skeleton down at me local MD, I said, I asked him to show me exactly where it was, and right at the bottom of the spine, there's these two big wings come out, under your arse, y'know, the cheeks of your arse. Well these two big wings come out like that, and they're full of holes, and all yer nerves are attached to 'em, to yer sacrum wings, and I had fractures to about, I think about four or five, I dunno. I got the x-ray and report at home, and all that sorta stuff, y'know. It just says fractures of the sacrum wings.

(SG40) They give you the questions, you just gotta tick off how you feel, y'know. It's quite good, quite simple. 'What do you think of the earthquake?' I just writ on the bottom, 'I just wanna forget all about it.' That's what I writ. Y'know, I just writ on the bottom, 'I just wanna forget all about the bloody earthquake.' That's it, y'know. Which I do really.

All storytellers step forward. They hold for a moment as the sounds of the Club fade up.

Blackout.

END OF ACT ONE

ACT TWO

SCENE THIRTEEN: JUMP CLUB

MELBA, STEFO, HOWARD, ELAINE, EDDIE, KERRY

Actors enter as sounds of the Club fade out. Focus on MELBA *alone.*

MELBA: (MM1) My name is Melba Middleby. I was a foundation member of the Club. 1948. And in 1949, I became the first woman on the Club's Board. I used to play piano with them to sing the... what... community singing, you know. And of course my husband Bob used to play the drums. Reg Abraham, he used to be in the... in the Fire Brigade. I don't know whatever happened to him. But he was the one who used to show the words, you know, the slides with the words... Elsie Anderson and Margaret Jeffries, they were the main two female singers. They had lovely voices. And Alan Williams, he lived at Boolaroo then, and he used to be the Secretary of the Plumbers, and he was another singer... he had a beautiful harmonising voice Alan. Elaine Richards, she used to work at the Club... one of the... like the barmaids, you know, and she had a lovely voice. Tex Smith... he was a funny little fellow... used to play an accordion, and Lora Strurl, she had a great voice too. She lived at Wickham. Don't know whether she still lives there. But then there was this other chap, I can't think of his... Barney Freeman... it just came to my mind... Barney Freeman. Oh he was funny. He was a really... wonderful comedian, Barney Freeman...

(MM2) When they gave us this commemorative membership badge, in April, 1989, it was lovely. You were all assembled, like you're all sitting down at these long tables. And I was thinking how lovely it was. And then we went out and we played the pokies for a while, and had a look around, and then... I think they had dancing on and that, you know that night too. I was thinking how lovely it was, you know. And to think that that's all rubble…

All come into focus.

STEFO: [*with great enthusiasm*] (SN16) Everyone went to the Club… basically it had the nicest atmosphere.

MELBA: (MM1) I felt that I could walk in and… that everybody was friendly, and nice… If you wanted to put a few bob in the pokies, you could do it.

STEFO: (SN22) Had good grog. Had good beer. You ask a Novocastrian… they're very fussy about their beer, right. So they had good beer.

HOWARD: (SN18) But it felt safe. No aggro. I never saw anyone tossed down the stairs, but I know there was. I know there were people tossed down the stairs.

KERRY: (KI15) One guy, this was years ago at the Club, and he's looking at me really seductive, and I said, 'Are you right there?', and he said, 'Can of draught'. And next thing you know, one of the bouncers come up, 'Don't give him that beer'. I said, 'What's the matter?' They picked him up both arms and he's got his dick hanging out… he was pissing up the bloody bar wall.

EDDIE: (ES23,24) It was everybody's central meeting place and office in the same place. Union delegate work, Trades Hall meetings, social life… How I got to know the place, because I used to show films there, and running 'round and finding out all… where all the power points were in these little rooms. We showed films about nuclear disarmament, and yeah, stuff like that, and held meetings there, and we had State Conferences there, and all that stuff.

MELBA: (MM1) I knew one woman who signed up as a boy in the early days. And she was on the roll as a boy for three years. Why? So they'd let her go on all the fishing trips up to the Club's hut at Fingal Bay.

HOWARD: (HG38) I've been a member of the Workers Club for twenty-five years. I've worked there for twenty-three. It goes back to the period when I was a very young person, and the Vietnam era. And I saw… I come from a conservative background, but I saw the activity within the Club… the action against the Vietnam War. And I sought out further to find out what was going on, and what made these people tick… And here's… here's, well… a Club full o' lefties… a club emanating from the trade union movement and the working class. And they're… you know… people who march on the street.

STEFO: (SN22) All the sort of lefty functions. They always happened there. Nowhere else.

EDDIE: (ES25) After the rallies we all used to go back to the Club for a drink, and May Days 'n' all that.

ELAINE: (JO4) They all said it was wonderful, from a social aspect… dances of a Wednesday, Friday night, Saturday night sometimes.

HOWARD: (JO4) As a matter of fact, when it was used for a private dance, they used to call it the 'Home Wreckers'.

KERRY: (KI14,16) And later the Jump Club, the Parachute Club… all the divorcées used to go there and they used to pick up a one-night stand… One night, years ago, when I was a casual, I was upstairs in Bar Five. This fellow come in, what, in his mid-fifties. He was looking for his 'daughter', and I said, 'Oh, if she comes in, she would be downstairs'. So he got his drink and he went over and he was looking over the balcony to see if he could find his 'daughter'. I was talking to some people I haven't seen in a long time, and having a yabba… and looked out and broke up with laughter. All I could see was the sole of his shoes, like this, going over the balcony. He bent over too far. And I'm going, 'No wonder they call it the bloody Jump Club… check him out'.

ELAINE: (EG38) A few years ago, the Club was constantly under quite subtle attacks from, from… you know, from outside. There was anti-communism, and anti-left, and pro-Christian. They got together and set about to try and destroy the Club. They never could… And we just couldn't imagine Newcastle without the Newcastle Workers Club. My dad was a foundation member of the Club, And I was always on the May Day floats… For the whole year after the quake, you could go down and see an empty thing. I wonder what Dad'd think. It was his whole life.

MELBA: (JO14,8) It's maybe foolish to say, but it's like losing a loved one, a great friend, or a loved member of your family, or something like that. It was a tremendous loss, and still is. You know the old saying, you never miss anything 'til you lose it.

◆ ◆ ◆ ◆ ◆

SCENE FOURTEEN: BARRIERS

EDDIE, JULIE

EDDIE: (ES1) I was in Fremantle… at the time of the quake, and we were loading a ship… with sheep of all things, and one of the other wharfies on the wharf said to me… who knew I was from Newcastle… said, 'Eddie there's been an earthquake in Newcastle'. And I just… 'Oh well, oh yeah, okay, it's a tremor'. You don't worry about those things.

(ES2) So after lunch we all went back to work. Another guy comes up to me and says, 'There's people trapped in the Workers Club', and I said, 'I'm gone. I'm outa here.' And so I went and seen the foreman, and he's aware of my situation… you know, I was connected to the Workers Club and I had friends and… relatives in Newcastle.

(ES5) I got my mate to take me out to the airport… very agitated, didn't know what was going on. I burst into tears at Perth Airport, and the airline had to fix me up, the whole bit… then [*laughing*] the plane broke down on the tarmac for four bloody hours. So in the interim I'm ringing up Newcastle and I got through to Elaine Gibson, Howard's wife. And she told me about Lenny and Barry being missing. And Lenny's been an old waterfront watchman… he's pretty close. I'd worked with him quite a bit. And Barry… I've got a lot of affection for… and, as a good bloke.

(ES6) So eventually I got away from Perth, and by this time it was obvious that I was going to miss my connecting flight… there was no other flights to Newcastle, so I tried to hire a car… every car company refused me a car to go to Newcastle… which really shitted me off… because of the earthquake. They wouldn't allow a car to go.

(ES7) The trains weren't running, as I found out… so I stayed at Mum's place that night. Next morning I flew up… and… I don't know… crazy me asked the pilot to fly over Newcastle, [*chuckling*] but he wouldn't. I said, 'Do us a favour and have a look', but he wouldn't.

He takes a deep breath.

(ES9) Tried to get around to the Workers Club… They wouldn't let me. Even though I told them who I was, they said, 'Bad luck'. Rang other people, got filled in on what was happening. Barry and Lenny was still missing. I think by that time the death toll out of the Club was about seven. I think.

(ES10) I was sort of in no man's land… just kept lookin' down towards the Club… couldn't realise it.

JULIE: (JPK7) I heard on the radio that you weren't allowed to enter the city, I was annoyed by that, and I can understand reasons for that, but I… it's like being cut off from someone who's ill… that you want to see, and you know that your presence might help them some way, and you're just not allowed to.

(JPK9) I went 'round all the side streets that I could, stupidly thinking… and then I drove as far into town as I could and got stopped before the Club… They were saying it wasn't at all safe, and I'd have to go back, and they'd be really pleased if I turned around and went the other way.

(JPK11) It was like having a wide shot of something, and what you really want is a close-up, you know. And all I could really think of was little bits of buildings in my head visually, like corners of windows, and I just wanted to be closer…

EDDIE: (ES11) I was walking along Hunter Street and there was no one around… The next minute this bum wagon pulls up and the copper's a bit aggro, and I said, 'It's all right, I'm just goin' for a walk', and he said, 'You've got to go back'.

JULIE: (JPK13) I'd start photographing from a few feet outside a barrier, and then get closer and closer and closer, and then sort of look around and see if I could jump inside the barrier and then see how far I could go until someone came. So for quite a long time there was the feeling of… yeah, being shut out, and also sneaking around like a kid and sort of… you know, going under fences and going over things. There was this… yeah just a constant thing of no-go areas, which to me reminds me of childhood things a lot.

EDDIE: (ES8) I was staying in the Cricketers Arms because my own place had been sub-let, and I'd booked in there and one day I went downstairs and immediately ran into a table of people that I knew and they started tellin' me some of the stories which… blew me out

Paul Makeham as Eddie and Kath Leahy as Julie in the 1991 WCAC production. (Photo: David Owens, WCAC)

of my tree actually… about the Workers Club, and by that time a lot more information had been revealed about what the staff did on the day of the quake.

◆ ◆ ◆ ◆ ◆

SCENE FIFTEEN: SERVICE INDUSTRY

WAYNE, JOHN, LYN, KERRY, MARG

WAYNE: (WD22) 'It has become apparent to me that amongst other things I've done in my life that there is a great deal of satisfaction to be gained personally from being involved in the service industry…' Wayne Dean, Club Secretary Manager, one year after the quake.

(WD1) December the twenty-eighth, 1989, I can recall feeling a shudder in the building… as if there was something outside my office... A band was going to play in the Club that evening, and they had a large semi-trailer parked outside. I'd thought well, they're going to unload shortly and they'll be bringing their gear in. Straight away in my mind I had it that this semi-trailer that I had observed that was parked in King Street had impacted the Club.

JOHN: (JC58) I told Wayne Dean it was an earthquake, and he said, 'Naaa'. I said, 'It was. It was. I'm tellin ya.' 'Na, shut up, John.' It's like he's sayin' you're only a cleaner, you don't know. [*Laughing*] 'Well fair enough.'

WAYNE: (WD1) I recall thinking, gee the damage by this truck is over the top... that it must have hit a most vital point of the Club, that it's, that it's caused this domino effect... And I recall that falling like confetti were the aluminium slats off the ceiling. Ten-metre long slats floating down like confetti, hundreds of them. Then it struck me that those slats belonged on the ceiling of the auditorium, the level above. They'd fallen right through two floors.

MARG: (MT20) Wayne stayed actually inside the Club, and he kept going back in. Endless times. You could see Wayne running in and out of the Club, rescuing people. And he kept saying, 'Do a head count. Do a staff count. See who's missing.'

WAYNE: (WD1) I remember being on the mezzanine floor amongst this chaos and leaning across, over the debris and seeing the people in the western side of the Water Board building standing there, looking at us, and I called out to these guys at the top of my voice to get some jacks. They felt a little helpless I suppose... There are a lot of other details that you sort of... it's become a bit of a blur... I can recall there was a lady in front of me who was hurt and an elderly gentleman... and I can recall helping them to the top of the floor and I told them to get out of the Club straight away. I wanted her to get out because I was afraid the rest of the place would fall. But the lady was insistent on sitting down and I was rather stressed by that and I was quite, I probably would have been close to being rude about her sitting there.

KERRY: (KI5) Wayne Dean made a comment to the other Kerry. Wayne turned 'round to her and said, 'I could have prevented this'.

LYN: (LB22) When I was brought out of the building, there was this old gentleman, older gentleman, and a lady and two children, that came through the crowd. I can remember the gentleman because they came right up beside me and I could hear him saying to the lady, 'Now pull yourself together. He is going to need you. He doesn't need to see you break down, because you gotta be strong for him.' And I didn't realise who it was, and then Wayne came out of the building, and it was his wife. And her father was really being quite hard on her, to be strong for Wayne, and Wayne walked over, he walked across the street and he was staggering, like he was drunk. Once he seen his family, he went to pieces, completely to pieces. He sorta slumped down onto the ground. He was only there a few minutes. They made sure he was all right. He made sure they were all right, and he went straight back inside the Club. I thought to myself, when he comes down, boy, he's gonna really collapse.

SCENE SIXTEEN: ADRENALIN

KERRY, MARG

KERRY *and* MARG *take up positions as at the end of Scene Seven: 'First Aid'.*

MARG: My uniform is all covered in blood.

KERRY: (MT13) Once the ambulances arrived, they threw bandages and whatever else at us, you know, anybody who knew how to tie a bandage was in.

MARG: (MT14) And people came from everywhere with jugs of water, and cups and things. They were washing people's mouths out, and washing their eyes out, and whatever…

KERRY: (MT14) And yet there was other people standing around just looking. Able-bodied men who were letting women carry other men, and you felt like grabbing some of them and shaking the hell out of them and saying, 'Get in there and do something', because the management and that, they wouldn't let the women back in.

MARG: (MT14) And they said to us, 'Stay out. Do what you can for everybody outside.' We just picked up whoever we could and got them across the street.

KERRY: (MT12) Marg and I picked this old man up. He was on his

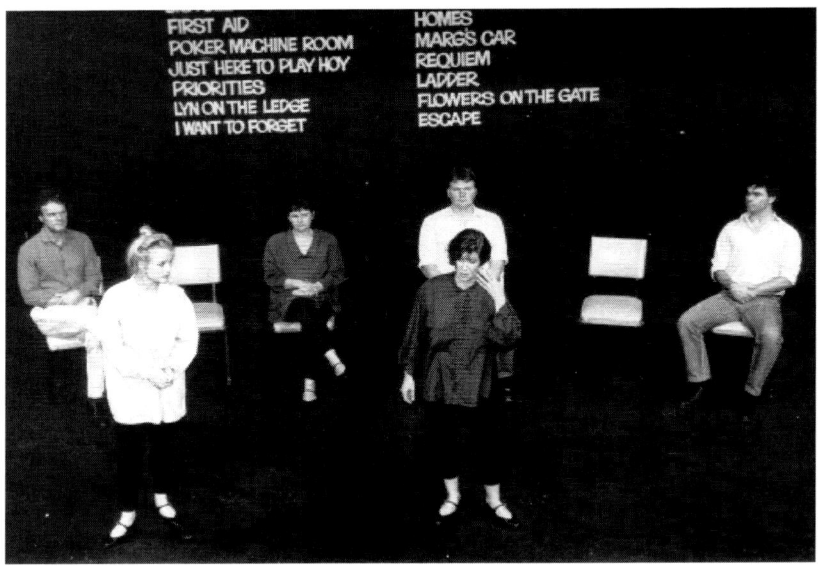

Sue Porter as Kerry and Rebecca Brandon as Marg in the 1991 WCAC production. (Photo: David Owens, WCAC)

hands and knees in front of the carpark entrance when we got to him.

MARG: (MT17) You know this man that Kerry and I picked up, he was a big man, he was well over six foot, and a solidly built bloke. Kerry and I bodily picked him, off his hands and knees. I mean you hear about things like that, and you just think it'll never happen with you, but we didn't think about it.

KERRY: (MT12) And he had this wound on the top of his head, and it was just sort of scraped back over the top of his head, and it just lifted the whole skin off, off the top of his head, and he was absolutely white, from head to foot… And he'd actually been standing in the poker machine room floor, and he'd gone through the floor, and through the carpark, and he was laying in the basement, to what we think, and he said he remembers looking up, [*laughing*] and the wheels of his own car were hanging over his head. And he's just laying there, and he thought, 'Christ, I'm going to get crushed to death with me own car', you know. And I remember laughing at him at the time.

MARG: (MT37) It's amazing what you can do when you have to. They talk about adrenalin and all of this sort of thing… You stand there and cry or scream or whatever else while you're doing it… it just… it just has to be done. I don't know where it all came from, but it did, at the right time, I suppose.

◆ ◆ ◆ ◆ ◆

SCENE SEVENTEEN: CELLAR LEVEL

ELAINE, JOHN, BOB

JOHN: (JC22) I've just got to cellar level, and there's a stairwell, and that stairwell there at the cellar it goes off to the side and then down, that goes off to the basement, and I've come down, and I've managed to… There's the lift, I've come around to the lift, and I could walk right up to where Barry's bench was, his bench was about there. And I just couldn't see his bench, I was about three feet in front of his bench, and I knew that he was just there. And I didn't know that anyone else was with him. I thought he could've been just by himself.

BOB: (BA12) I said to one of the rescue blokes, I think there could be a bloke downstairs. 'Cause I hadn't seen him.

(BA12) And we went down there and the emergency fella sang out. We couldn't see nothin'. He moved in a bit further, and I wasn't going any further. I could see it was… you could see it all just hanging there, and he went underneath, and shouted and sang out… There was no reply. Pitch black, and he said, 'Well if they're alive', he said, 'they're not here'.

JOHN: (JC22) And I had a… I had a… I had a fireman with me at the time. I said, 'There's a guy just there'. He says, 'Righto'.

BOB: (BA12) So we give it away and went back upstairs. And the police sorta moved us all, any workers, like any people belonging to the Club, moved us all back, and 'your services are no longer required'.

ELAINE: (EG11) And as we'd been coming home, I saw this car that my friend... that our friend's car was there. And I said, 'That's Lenny's car'. He always parks his car there, and goes for the poker machines... and he plays the poker machines at the Club. And I thought, 'Lenny's in there'.

◆ ◆ ◆ ◆ ◆

SCENE EIGHTEEN: JENNY

JENNY, JOHN

JOHN: (JC62) I've gone to the basement, and then all of a sudden this girl's come up, one of the girls from work experience, and she's gone, 'John! John! Jennifer's down there. Go help her. Go find her. She's in there somewhere.' And I've gone, 'Nooo'. I've known Jennifer for years. I used to give her heaps as a kid. I used to throw rocks at her and things like that... so I've gone in looking for her.

JENNY: (JM16) I knew John Constable a long time ago. He'd lived in Stockton and then I hadn't seen him for years and then I come to do my work experience at the Workers Club, and I met up with him again, and then we had a lot of memories of Stockton and that.

JOHN: (JC14) She's under there...

JENNY: (JM5,6) I'm pinned by a slab of something and I just don't know what's going on... I can't get myself out... and I'm pinned by a pokie. It's come down and is staring me in the face.

(JM9,10) I am having a slight asthma attack... and my asthma spray has fallen out, so I have no asthma spray to calm me down, and so I'm just talking myself out of having the attack. All I want to do is to go to sleep...

JOHN: (JC14) All they can see is just a little bit of her head. And I see this little gap about this wide. And I stick my head down, crawl down face first, and I'm totally right up to me ankles into this rubble before I get to her. And then this SES guy just grabs me by the ankles and just holds me, you know... and I get to her, and I start caressin' her, 'How ya goin Jennifer? What are you up to? What

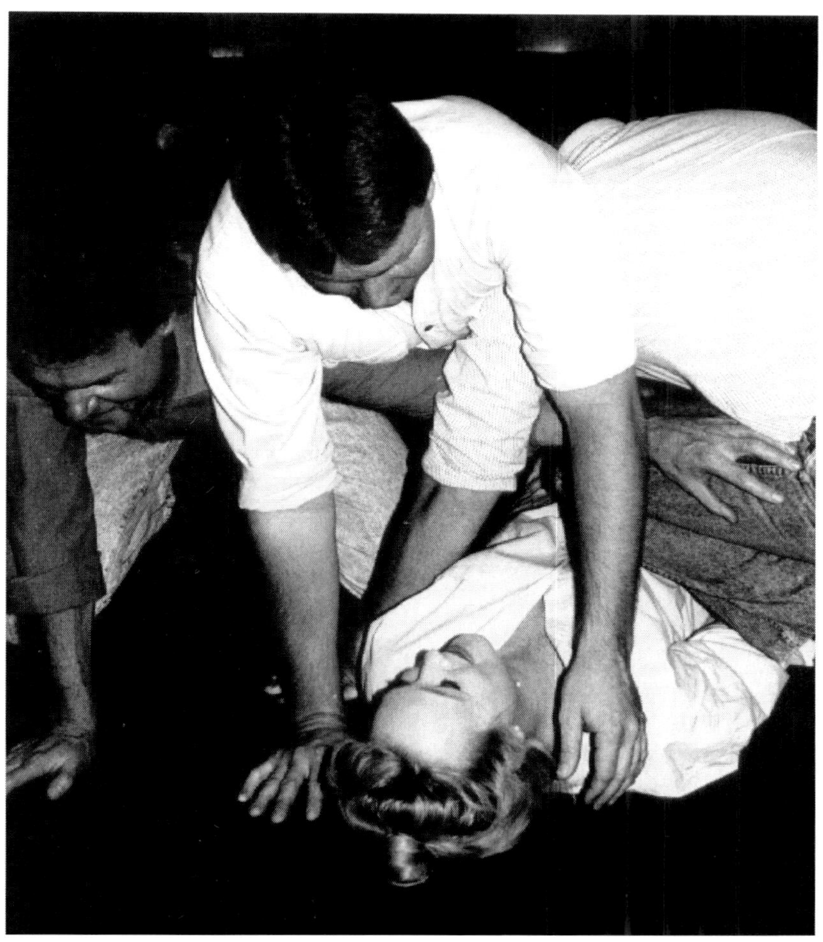

David Cameron as John and Sue Porter as Jenny in the 1991 WCAC production. (Photo: David Owens, WCAC)

are you doing down here? What's happening?' [*He laughs.*] 'You tell me what's happening.' 'I don't know what's happening either. I've come to help ya.'

JENNY: (JM6) I can feel electrical cables 'round me leg. It's all 'round me ankle under the slab.

JOHN: (JC14) I go straight down, and I go right under, so I can reach me hand straight up underneath to her ankle.

(JC15,16,17,18) And I feel all it was was her shoelace, so I'm sayin', 'It's okay, Jen, it's only your shoelace. It's all right.' She says, [*making a big sigh*] 'Oh…' A big sigh comes out of her head. And they pass down these jaws, and I put it underneath the brick… well, it wasn't brick, it was a whole slab. I'm comin' in from that way, and they're digging from this side… They're gonna start cutting the door out. 'If you cut the door out, everything's gonna collapse on her…' And then this, I don't know who he is, he's a yobbo anyway. I'm sayin', 'Her leg's clear'. And this SES guy says, 'The leg's not clear', and I'm saying, 'Her leg's clear, there is nothing on it at all. Her foot's clear, I can move her foot.' And this guy says, 'No, her leg's not clear…' Anyway, he's put another jaws in on the other side… but as he's lifting it it's unstable, and I can see it gonna go, and I grab the slab, and as I try to hold the slab, 'crunch', and the whole thing just falls straight back down on her leg. 'OH'… tryin' to hold onto her leg, [*miming the action, reliving the effort*] and she's just letting out this almighty scream, you know, and I go, 'Oh no', I say, 'Quick, get it back under there', and he puts it back under there… And anyway, he's lifting it back up straight away, and he gets it off her leg, and he says, 'Oh, her leg's clear now'. [*Laughing knowingly at the stupidity of the yobbo*] 'Her leg was clear the first time.' And he says, 'We're gonna drag her out, and as we drag her out, you straighten the leg, and then support it as it's comin' out…' [*Cynically*] Right… 'Oh, here we go', and he starts just draggin' her out, she's a bit frantic to start, see. And I've started straightenin' out her leg and… and as I'm straightening out her leg, I go to about there [*indicating on his own leg*] and she starts [*mimicking her guttural scream*], 'Ahhh…' 'It's okay, Jen, in five minutes, you're not gonna feel a thing, you won't have nothin' to worry about. It's all right. It's okay.'

JENNY: Yeah, okay.

JOHN: (JC14) She says [*mimicking her gentle tone of resignation*], 'Yeah, okay', sort of calmin' herself down again.

(JC19) And the SES guy let her leg… leg drop. I can't believe it, I'm yellin' up to him, 'What are you doin'?' and he's just grabbed me by the legs. He just wants me out of there. And he's gone 'rip', and I've got scratches all up me arms, all up me guts, and… rips me shirt. [*He amuses himself with this part of the story.*] He shakes me hand… this is the good one, he shakes me hand and he says, 'Ar… Well done, mate'.

JENNY: (JM22) I am very dry. All I want is a drink of water, and a spit. I've got so much dirt in my mouth and in my throat that I've swallowed all the dust that… the smelly dust, and it is such a very hot day…

JOHN: (JC68) Ah, me mouth. The sensation of dryness in my mouth is unbelievable. I mean I can't even talk. It is hard to talk… because I am shakin' that much, my hand is just like this… it's unbelievable just how much I'm shaking.

(JC66) And straight after that, this doctor comes 'round saying, 'Morph, pethadene, morph, morph, anyone want some?' I'm sitting there… 'Mmmmm'.

JENNY: (JM20) John turned around and said, 'Well Jen, I've got to go and get more people out. I'll see you after.' I said to him, 'Well all right, come and see me'.

JOHN: (JC65) She's crying, 'Come and visit me in the hospital'… 'Ah yeah, no worries…'

JENNY: But he never got there.

JOHN: (JC65) I never saw her. [*Laughing*] I hate hospitals. They smell.

SCENE NINETEEN: HOMES

JOHN, HOWARD *and* ELAINE, FAY *and* BOB, LYN, WAYNE

Focus on JOHN, *quite angry.*

JOHN: (JC67) I'd been under for two and a half, three hours. By that time there was a mass of people everywhere. I went back up inside and all the tills were… and the only people up there were the fire, SES ambulance and police… and I mean that till I pulled off her.. probably three hundred, four hundred dollars in it. It was empty, not a cent in it. And the money we pulled off her. One dollars, ten cents, especially all the notes. I thought it just goes to show there's some people got just enough time to fill their pockets while they go help someone.

(JC68) I shook me head, you know, and said 'fuckwits' and thought these guys know what they're doin', [*laughing*] I guess I'll leave. So I walked out the door, you know, still shaken up, still swearin' me head off. Like a good night on the drink.

(JC69) I've walked back to where everyone was and a copper was saying, 'No, no, no you can't go through'. I've said, 'Listen mate, we just come out of there. I work in the place', and he said, 'Na, na. It's dangerous in there. People have been hurt…'

WAYNE: (WD32) It was decided on the advice of police that we should move to Civic Park, and about ten to two we met in the shade of the trees there, somewhere open and fairly safe… and we realised who wasn't there, who was missing. I told the staff that the rescue effort would continue. We weren't prepared at that stage to give up. And I told the staff that if they could find their way home to do so. There were quite a few people whose… whose cars were in the Club and who'd lost their vehicles. I said, 'Could you please make your own way home, because we just can't arrange anything at this time'.

LYN: (LB30) It had come over the radio that there'd been one killed in the administration office… and I suddenly thought, it suddenly struck me, you know… my children, you know. It wasn't… I didn't think it was happening outside Newcastle. I thought this was it. It was just the Club… She was virtually just beside herself, my daughter. When I finally got through, she answered the phone. I said, 'Amanda, it's Mum', and she… I can remember her saying, 'Are you all right? Are you all right?' You know, and I… virtually… that's when I broke down… You know, I'm usually a fairly hard person… but that's when it finally hit me, you know, that there could have possibly been not a time when I was going to ring her, and let them know that I was okay. And she said that she'll get Dad to come in and pick me up.

JOHN: (JC24) I thought well, no one knows I'm alive yet, 'cause I heard on the radio as I was out the front, they had a radio goin', and one of them said, 'Fifty dead at the Workers Club…' and I thought, 'How do they know that?', you know? It was the Sydney media that said that, it wasn't the local media, and so I thought, 'Oh, maybe they think I'm dead'.

He laughs.

(JC24,72) I've just sort of decided, right there and then, because I saw a car go past that I knew, just hailed them over and I said, 'Take me home'. And they took me halfway home, and I ran the rest of the way, and I just got big cuddles and kisses when I got there, 'Ohhh, glad you're alive'. Me girlfriend's bawling her eyes out, me mum's bawling her eyes out. Me sister's bawling her eyes out. They're all just bawling. I was going, 'Give us a break, did you think I was gonna die? More than an earthquake to get me down mate.' They're all sort of happy for a while. Me girlfriend wouldn't leave me side all day, and I couldn't leave the phone all day 'cause she was runnin' hot. 'Yeah, I'm alive', ding, 'I'm alive', ding, 'I'm alive'.

WAYNE: (WD39) I went home… and checked my own house out, and at that point I, I discovered how badly damaged it was. I started to see significant cracks in the walls, but I was so concerned about what had happened at work my home situation became a secondary thought, and I went back to the Club. I didn't go home that night until midnight. By that time the rescue had gone into full scale effort around the clock.

LYN: (LB31) When I got home I… did nothing. Just sat. Stunned I think was the word. And then just got up and went around my daily duties. You know, like I normally would do when I got home. Cooked tea, just did the normal things, cooked tea, and then virtually sat back down again, watched a bit of the TV, and… found it very difficult to sleep, to go to bed, to unwind, to go to sleep, yes… and that went on for a long time.

Focus on HOWARD *and* ELAINE *as a couple.*

ELAINE: (EG12) I think Howard was in shock. He couldn't talk because of the broken ribs… And we were still frightened to come into the house, because everyone was waiting for this second earthquake.

HOWARD: (HG36) I kept thinking of the aftershock. I've always heard about earthquakes, but having never experienced one, like most of us, I've always heard about aftershocks. Sometimes they're nearly as bad as the actual shock.

ELAINE: (EG7) Everyone had said, 'Oh, don't go back inside the house'. And it was a terrible hot day, so we'd sat out in the back lane.

(EG12) It was scary that night. You had the army on one corner, the police on the other. I felt something bad was going to happen. We sat up all night. Didn't speak much. We were sort of waiting for a report on the TV to tell us what to do. I felt sorry for people with little kids... would they put their kids to bed that night. No one seemed to know what to do to get through the night. So we just sat in the lounge room.

Focus on FAY *and* BOB *as a couple.*

FAY: (FA/BA22) [*merry*] Well, the door... Our front door rattled...

BOB: And I felt the bed go.

FAY: And I sat up and I screamed, and I said, 'What was that?', and Bob said, 'I think we've just had another one'... 'cause he felt the bed go, but I didn't feel the bed go.

BOB: And I went back to sleep.

FAY: And I laid awake.

BOB: Fay laid awake all night.

FAY: Couldn't breath, I was hyperventilating. He said, 'You all right?' I said, 'Yeah'. But Bob just went back to sleep then.

◆ ◆ ◆ ◆ ◆

SCENE TWENTY: MARG'S CAR

MARG

MARG: (MT1) Barry used to call me 'Little Passion Flower', which I thought was lovely... It was just something Barry used to make up... He'd call you anything, something that always had a... a meaning to Barry. He was actually cleaning the doors when I went into work that day, and... he said to me, 'Hello my little passion flower'. And I said, 'How are you, Barry?' and he said, 'Never seen the world so bright'. And that was at ten o'clock, about five to ten, that day.

(MT44) The police rang me, I think on the Saturday, no it must have been the Friday, Friday afternoon... and they said that they'd got cars out, of the Club, and would I go in to the McDonald's carpark and see if my car was one of them. So I got my ex-husband to drive me in, and it was eerie, it really was, incredible.

(MT46) I said to the policeman, 'Is it badly damaged, my car?' He said, 'Well, put it this way darlin', if you've got a foot ruler, you won't need it all'. And I thought, 'Oh... God'. And when I went and had a look at it... the man at the towing service didn't actually want to show it to me. He wasn't going to let me in the yard. He said to me, 'Look, your husband and your kids can go', he said. ' That's fine', he said, 'But I don't think you should go'. And I said to him, 'No', I said, 'I need to go. I need to have a look at it.' And you couldn't tell it was a station wagon. My tyres were shredded. It had no roof left on it. The floor was actually sitting where the roof should have been.

She laughs.

(MT47) It was... To think that it was on top of where everybody was. Because I'd reversed my car into the back of the western wall that day, in the carpark. I was about two spaces from the end of the entrance. And I overheard one of the rescue men saying that that was where they found Barry, was under that side of the wall, and that really shook me up to think that my car was actually on top of Barry.

SCENE TWENTY-ONE: REQUIEM

EDDIE

EDDIE: (ES12,13,14) Sunday I woke up in the pub... I was told there was going to be a function for all the staff on New Year's Eve, and I just couldn't understand how anyone could do it. And I went for a walk...

Paul Makeham as Eddie in the 1991 WCAC production. (Photo: David Owens, WCAC)

there was nothing else to do… just waiting for information… and [*laughing*] I walked down Darby Street towards Civic Park, and there was a copper at Tyrell Street, and she said, 'You can't go past here'. I said, 'Look, I only want to sit in the park and read the paper'. So I 'read the paper' for 'bout an hour and a half… I went to the Commonwealth and had a beer and just said hello to a few people. Then I walked down to the Cricketers Arms and two coppers walked in… a male and a female… and I said… 'Have they found Barry and Lenny yet?', and they asked me their last names and she turned around and said, 'Yeah, they pulled them out a four a.m. this morning'. And with that I sort of cracked up and went outside and just sort of cried to myself. And… well then… it was a relief in one way because they knew they were both dead. So that night I went over to the New Year's Eve party, and saw all the people. And everyone was there, bar a few. Even Glen Sparks was there… whose father was found at four a.m.… which I thought was rather courageous on his behalf.

(ES18) After that, you'd be talking to people in the street… the people walking around with 'Where were you?' on the T-shirts and that stuff. 'I survived the 5.5'… and… our staff were getting counselling, which was great.

He exhales loudly.

(ES15) Unfortunately a conflict arose in terms of the times of Lenny's and Barry's funeral. They were both on the same day at the bloody same time… so one had to make the choice, and I went to Lenny's… which wasn't so formal… 'cause Lenny being an old… member of the Party, and all that. Blokes… people came from Port Kembla and everything… for his funeral, which was great.

(ES16) And we found out something about Lenny we didn't know… Lenny was a great collector of classical music. And I didn't know, and I used to talk to Lenny about a lot of things, but that's one thing none of us knew.

◆ ◆ ◆ ◆ ◆

SCENE TWENTY-TWO: LADDER

JOHN, LYN

JOHN: On the day the earthquake struck, Lyn Brown was trapped up in her office for forty minutes. To John Constable it felt like five minutes.

LYN: The story of Lyn Brown's rescue.

JOHN: (JC8) I ran up around past the Bistro and up the back fire escape, which go... leads to Bar Four, and anyway, soon as I got to the top of the fire escape, the first set, the fire escape, there was nothing. Bar Four was not there. And Lyn was on the next flight up. And I've gone, 'Oh no', and I looked up and there's this small little pigeon hole, and that's where Lyn's office was. I came up the fire escape there, and it broke off along there. There was just a very thin little ledge.

(JC55) And I've gone, 'Oh fuck no. Fuck, fuck, fuck, fuck, fuck...' [*Laughing*] I've gone, 'Lyn'... just a wail, and she's gone [*mimicking her whimper*], 'Yes'. 'Where are ya?' I've looked up and here's this little pigeon hole and she's just popped her head over then and gone [*mimicking her soft voice*], 'Help'. 'Stay there. Stay there.'

LYN: (LB28) [*laughing*] He was swearing... and that... John doesn't do that, normally, particularly in front of me, because he knows I'd give him a smack for it. I couldn't see him, see. I could only hear him, underneath me, right down the bottom... and I yelled out to him, 'John, you're swearing!' 'Oh sorry', he said.

JOHN: (JC56) And I've looked down, and these two Water Board guys were movin' away with a ladder, and I've whistled out and I said, 'Hey, hey, give me that ladder up here'.

(JC10) So what we've ended up doing, was there was rubble, all here... ended up putting just the legs of it into the rubble, and one of the Water Board guys just sat there with his hands into the rubble, and we tracked it up to Lyn's office, and the other one put all his weight behind the ladder, got up on that slight ledge and put all his weight behind the ladder,

LYN: (LB6) They virtually just held it in mid-air, and John climbed the ladder, with the guys holding it, and he jumped over into my office,

Kath Leahy as Lyn and David Cameron as John in the 1991 WCAC production. (Photo: David Owens, WCAC)

and just grabbed hold of me. Don't ask me how I got over to the ladder, but I had to get over to the ladder…

(LB26) And he just kept on talking, going from one thing to another. He was still very hyped up, but when he reached me he seemed to settle a little bit more. He probably felt that the shoe was on the other foot… at the moment he was probably able to do something for me for a change.

JOHN: (JC57) I said, 'I'll go first and you can come down sort of in front of me'. Anyway, she's… I've gone down, and she couldn't get down fast enough. [*Laughing*] I thought I was gonna go right up her skirt.

LYN: (LB7) And John manoeuvred me down this ladder, and they said, 'Step out onto this ledge'. I put one foot out, and then the ledge went, so I had to get back on the ladder, and we went down a bit further… that's where they jammed the door in, between the carpet and some rubble. And a workman was standing behind that, and I had to jump over to the… to the door, and so he had his arms out, you know, and it was only a little space that I had to jump over to.

(LB9) And all of a sudden I saw these stairways sticking out from nowhere. I had to jump around onto that, then. And then John followed me down the ladder. He followed me down the ladder, and he just… when we got halfway down the stairs, you know, he just sorta grabbed hold of me, and sort of, you know, went to pieces.

JOHN: (JC11) She give me a big cuddle, and I give her a cuddle, a pretty tight one.

He laughs, and enacts breathing heavily in the cuddle.

(JC60) I'm sittin there cuddlin' her and we were walking down past the kiosk, I mean Bistro… and she says, 'Is anyone hurt?', and I said, 'No, not that I know of'.

LYN: (LB10) We got through the Club. He wouldn't let me look at anything. You know, he sort of covered me head, while we went through. But the only thing I do remember seeing was money. Just money everywhere when we got to the doorway of the Club.

(LB35) I waded through it as I was coming out… ten-cent, twenty-cent coins they would have been, and there was a lot of them, you know, scrunching under yer feet.

JOHN: (JC61) I've got her out and they're still pulling out people, and I'm in the middle of the street, and they're saying, 'Just stay here John, you've done your job. Just stay here.' 'There's still people screaming in there.'

He laughs.

Focus on LYN *alone.*

LYN: (LB30) He took me right out to the street. I can remember walking out of the front doors, and then I was swamped, by people… arms around you… and John just quietly slipped away, he must have because I don't remember seeing him. I know now that he went back in. Back inside the Club.

◆ ◆ ◆ ◆ ◆

SCENE TWENTY-THREE: FLOWERS ON THE GATE

LYN, KERRY, HOWARD, ELAINE, EDDIE, FAY, BOB, JENNY, JULIE

Focus on LYN *alone.*

LYN: (LB17) I remember up at Civic Park, Wayne was talking to the staff about what was going to happen, and it suddenly… suddenly it just struck me… Oh gee, I'm not going to work tomorrow. Up to that moment I honestly thought I was going to work the next day and I was gonna clean it all up. I didn't think how I was going to do it, I just knew I had to. And I thought, 'You fool', you know, but it was just the thing. I went there every day. It was just a part of my life. You know, when it suddenly struck me that there is no Club there… I was lost. I really was lost, and I just couldn't imagine…

Focus on all.

EDDIE: (ES20) We were still going to work… sounded really crazy… we were working on the waterfront and here's the city been devastated by an earthquake. And here are we still loading cargo and unloading cargo… I mean life seemed normal there… You only had to walk across the railway lines and it wasn't.

JULIE: (JPK14) It was very quiet, very grey and all the buildings were wrapped up in the green… whatever that stuff's called. And so it looked like big… ships. It just reminded me of big ships that had run aground, and they were sort of tatty ships too, they'd had a really bad time at sea.

EDDIE: (ES17) Finally I got to walk into the Club… We went in through with management. The older section was still standing. The demolishers had been in to a degree and had knocked down some of it. There was grog stacked up everywhere. No electricity. Then you walked to one section and here's this gigantic gap… in the floor… and there's the rest of the… the Club and, I mean poker machines down in the rubble, and all different types of things in the rubble.

JENNY: (JM6) I never knew until the sixth of January that I landed in the basement…

(JM27) The staff took me into the old Workers Club. I went down in the basement and I stood exactly where I landed… I stood for about five minutes. And it was something I had to do. It was an eerie feeling to have, sort of where I landed. And like where I did land there was still wires there and things from poker machines there.

(JM29) I always refer to the earthquake as an accident… I don't refer to it as an earthquake… it just sounds better… because when you tell people you were in the earthquake, they instantly feel sorry for you and say, 'Oh, you poor thing, you must've gone through hell…' Yes, I did go through hell for a little while, but now I just want to get on with life.

(JM29) But that site does something for me… that Union and King Street site. I was over there a few weeks before the anniversary, and I fell over on the street, right in that site… corner of Union and King Streets. I just fell over.

(JM30) My elbow was bleeding, but I wasn't worried about that. I was just feeling stupid to fall over… just there.

LYN: (LB43) When I looked at it, I thought, 'Now I could have gone down there'. It wouldn't have worried me to go down there. You know, if there was someone there who needed help, I would have liked to have helped.

FAY: (FA36) When we come back to work, when we got back to the temporary club we're in now, and we saw all the Hoy ladies again… she got me… the first day of the Hoy, the lady I'd sworn at on the footpath came back, and she said, 'Well, I don't have to pay for my board, because I never got me dollar back on the day the Club fell down'.

HOWARD: (HG41) I never walk into a building, or a major carpark, without looking up and saying, 'If it comes again, which is the way out?' And that's true, like particularly big shopping centres, where there's lots of carparks, and big heavy slabs of concrete. I can still see them as clear as they were, in a similar situation as the Workers Club. Big slabs of concrete falling down. And that sticks in your mind.

ELAINE: (EG23) Howard's not religious. And I'm supposed to be religious, but I'm not very good at it. So I have to believe that... it wasn't meant to... If it had happened that night, there could have been two thousand people there. And I would have been there... sitting in the kiosk, and I would have gone. And I was so lucky to have Howard. I couldn't hug him, and I couldn't kiss him for a whole week, you know. It was... it was as if I was so frightened to have nearly lost him.

KERRY: (KI26) There's times when my husband's at work in the mine, and the kids are in bed, and I'm reading a book, and I'm visualising the lounge room walls coming in. And the next day on the news you hear there's an earthquake somewhere in the world. And it really freaks me out.

(KI33) What amazed me is all our regular drunks, they all survived. And we don't know how we are going to be when we set foot in the new club. The old club is gone. You set foot on the new club. Same place. You don't know how you're going to be. We can't say 'til it's finished and you walk in there. All the ones that were on duty that day feel the same way.

ELAINE: When the new club opens, we'll go in there and work for a week and then we'll have the Grand Opening. We'll need that week... we have to check that the beer flows... and check all the seats in the Bistro are safe to sit on.

LYN: (LB24) Afterwards I carried all their burdens, each and every one of them. So did some of the other girls. The men don't like to see themselves probably in a role of talking to people like that.

(LB25) And Wayne'll take you up, and he'll say, 'Just try and handle it, Lyn', knowing you'll walk out and try.

EDDIE: (ES29) The anniversary in Civic Park. It was good... in the sense that a lot of people turned up to remember... the only thing about *that* was... I felt it my duty to go to *that* as a Director of the Club,

David Cameron as John in the 1991 WCAC production. (Photo: David Owens, WCAC)

to represent the Club at a public gathering, whereas my heart was with the people who were at the old club site… That's where I rather would've been.

FAY: We had a little ceremony on the old site.

BOB: Just the workers.

FAY: Elaine Gibson organised some flowers, and we just went in, a few of the staff, and just put them on the gate, and just had a little…

BOB: A minute's silence.

FAY: Yeah, no one said anything. There's not much to say really. You just had your own thoughts, and… that's all they did. And we just came away. But we didn't go to the Civic one, the Civic Park one, did we?

BOB: No, it didn't interest us.

FAY: We've shed our tears, and that's it.

ELAINE: (EG21) We kept the posies small and only put in a dollar each, knowing that flowers at that time of year would be difficult to get anyway. Two young boys came up from Sydney to lay flowers at the gate on the day of the anniversary. They were about twenty, twenty-two years old. They'd been drinking in the Club on the day the earthquake hit, but otherwise had no connection with the Club. They'd made the trip especially to be there, and they put their flowers on the gate with the workers.

Focus on LYN *alone.*

LYN: (LB41) John Constable wasn't there at the anniversary, and I was so, so very amazed at that. Well, we didn't see John. Whether he was there somewhere… And he came in the other day, to tell me he was going away. He needed to go away and try something new. I probably, from the experience of my own children going away, I knew that it would do him good. Give me a big cuddle and told me to look after… you know, and I said to look after himself… I felt like one of my own children was gone…

SCENE TWENTY-FOUR: ESCAPE

JOHN

JOHN: (JC73) Sunk the piss, mate. Straight onto the piss. I sank piss for seven days straight. I mean I did not sober up. I mean I woke up in the morning, and I'd sink piss again. I was… for some reason too scared to face what happened, and what I had gone through. And then the seventh day or the seventh night, I'd said, 'Ah, fuck this. I'm going out back for a spew.' You know. I was a changed person. I was more arrogant, more short tempered. Just pissed off with everything. Anyone tried to hassle me out… 'Fuck you'… straight up 'em, you know. And on the seventh day I'd… went out the back and just sat down and thought about it, and then bawled me eyes out… first time I'd cried in years. And really hit me like a ton of shit, eh? It all just came down all over me, like a sheet, and that was it. Bawled, and bawled and bawled. Then I stopped drinkin'. I felt a lot better… Then the eighth day I went to help work… and worked for a week. It was disgusting. Cleaning out the food and that and after seven days it went bad without any refrigeration.

(JC74) I think they wanted me to go back in for stress. They thought,

Jeremy Sims as John in the 1993 Belvoir St production. (Photo: Paul Wright)

like a horse, if you fall off, you should jump straight back on.

(JC75) Since the quake I've gone stir fucking crazy or whatever. Since the quake I've lost me girlfriend. She was a bitch anyway. [*Laughing*] I was under the thumb too much.

(JC76) Everyone's saying, 'Have you seen a counsellor?', and all this sort of shit. And I went and saw a female counsellor and all that sort of stuff. It was the second week. Acted like a real dag.

She must have thought I was really fucking crazy. I won't tell ya what I tried to do, no way. [*Laughing*] No. It's sick. But anyway it was so sick.

(JC70) I remember me and Wayne Dean are both running for the truck at the same time saying, 'A, a, a, a', like this. And Wayne Dean was closer than I was, and he's sort of turned around and seen it. I was in mid-stride, and Wayne Dean, he's come right up shouting and stopped it just before it ran over her head. 'A'. It was unbelievable. And we got the ambo driver that was just about to run over her head, we got him to take her away.

(JC77) I was talking to this male doctor and he was just talkin' about the war, and what he'd seen, and I'm tellin' him what happened with the quake. I said, 'Well, mate, I'm right into self preservation, but another thing is, I hate pain. I dunno, made me brain work overtime, and I really wanted to help.' He said, 'Look, [*with a smile*] I wish there were more boys like you around these days'... 'Thanks Dad.'

He laughs.

(JC78) I dreamt that all the graders and excavators and all that were... as they were pulling down walls... there was other parts falling down where people were.

(JC79) And I dreamt that I'd found the core of the earthquake. It was in the basement of the Workers Club. What it was was just this deep hole. I'd got all the bosses together and I said, 'Listen, this is where the earthquake comes', and they've gone, 'Bull'. And I've gone, 'Shhh, you'll have to keep quiet. If you talk too loud it'll start an earthquake.' They've gone, 'John, John, we want you to prove it'. And I've started down into this hole, and it's rumbled [*making a rumbling sound*] everywhere, and I've just darted into this little tunnel I knew come up near the door, the Union Street door. And my girlfriend's there. And I've said, 'What are you doing here? You're not supposed to be here.' And anyway I've gotten her out. And that was it... I'd found the core of the quake... And I'd just left all the bosses in the middle of the Club and I'd escaped my own way.

THE END

APPENDIX

Letter of agreement about a taped interview
Name:...
Address:...
Phone:...

The Workers Cultural Action Committee (WCAC) is a sub committee of Newcastle Trades Hall Council. It aims to provide cultural activities for workers and their families.

In 1991 WCAC will present a performance about the Newcastle Earthquake, that will draw on the experiences of people associated with the Workers Club, and others who have stories to tell about the earthquake and its aftermath.

As part of the research for the project, WCAC is interviewing a number of people on tape, and we thank you for contributing your taped interview. WCAC needs your permission to transcribe the interview, and make appropriate use of it in the following ways:

1. As background research material for a play.
2. As speeches to be included verbatim in a script for a play, and spoken by actors during a stage performance. Note: the speeches will need to be edited for this purpose.
3. As part of an archive of material to be kept by WCAC, for the use of genuine researchers and historians.
4. As part of an archive to be kept by public libraries and other organizations with oral history collections throughout Australia.
5. For broadcast on radio within a program about the earthquake.
6. For publication in a book.

Please delete any of the above uses that you do not want to authorize.

____

I agree to my interview being used in the above ways.

I also agree that copyright in the material will be owned jointly by myself and the interviewer, and that such copyright is licensed to WCAC and the Writer for the project, Paul Brown, for the uses listed above.

I do/do not give my permission for my name to be attributed to extracts from the transcripts or recordings involving myself and the interviewer.

I will receive a copy of the transcript of the interview.

I will be consulted by WCAC about any use of the material other than listed above.

Signed .... (Interviewee)

on............................ (date)

Countersigned...(Interviewer)

on.............................(date)